FREEDOM
to Be Me

Tools for Happiness,
Fulfilment and Peace

Dear Georgina
Lovely to Reconnect.
Hope you find Something
that Helps you to be 'You'
love Azmina
xx

AZMINA JIWA

Mark Shelmerdine has granted the author permission
to refer to the work of Susan Jeffers in this book. Dawn
Breslin has granted permission for the author to utilize her
acclamations in this book. Sheryl Andrews has granted
permission for the author to utilize parts of her book, *Manage
Your Critic*. Susan Hawkins has granted permission for use
of quotes from Dr David Hawkins' book, *Power vs. Force*.

Author photographs courtesy of Lauren M. Gezurian.
Page 9 photograph courtesy of Salim Jiwa.

Printed in the United Kingdom

First Printing, 2018

ISBN 978-1-9996315-8-1 (Print)
ISBN 978-1-9996315-9-8 (eBook)

Librotas Books
Portsmouth, Hampshire
PO2 9NT

www.Librotas.com

This book is dedicated to

My children Jazzmin and Shamir – For being my greatest inspiration to my personal growth.

My grandkids Kai and Vito – For allowing me to practise what I have learnt.

To all the children of the world – May they have the freedom to be themselves.

Praise for Freedom to Be Me

I had the privilege of working with Azmina as she unravelled her wisdom from her head and put it down on paper. I was inspired by the courage and strength of what at first might seem a small, quiet and meek woman. But as her story unfolded and her key learning points were divulged my heart expanded both in admiration for her and her journey but also in compassion for myself. I found myself becoming more aware of my own emotions, acknowledging them and then letting them go. As I read the activities I was instantly able to apply them in the moment and get instant results. If you feel you have lost a sense of who you are and what you want then *FREEDOM to Be Me* is a must-read.

Sheryl Andrews, The Strength and Solution Detective, Step by Step Listening

Azmina's book will help you unravel exactly what it is that is stopping you from being happy, being yourself, by challenging and changing the thoughts and beliefs which stop you from being the real you. Easy to read and packed with personal tried and tested examples, *FREEDOM to Be Me* is highly relatable. It is a nurturing book which will prove that anyone can make positive changes to their lives if they have the desire and commitment.

Samantha Wade, BMedSc, MSc, Team Leader

Azmina Jiwa's book, *FREEDOM to Be Me*, is both a personal and professional reflection of how to move forward towards a life you desire. Chapter by chapter with both practical exercises and personal reflections, Azmina lays out a game plan for those who may seem *'stuck in a rut'*, or living a life where challenges have become larger than personal accomplishments. Having known the author for twenty-five years I have seen in actuality how using the tools she shares in *FREEDOM to Be Me* have worked for her own life. From growing more confident and independent, to being able to coach others, the comprehensive list of simple reflection and action exercises has the possibility to assist any individual. For those who need to either begin, resume or just continue their personal journey, *FREEDOM to Be Me* can assist in accomplishing the goals one needs to create a happy and balanced life.

Lauren M. Gezurian, Educational Consultant & Teacher

FREEDOM to Be Me, it says it in the title. This book is one of the most powerful books I have read; it really spoke to my true inner self. This book, if read chapter by chapter, taking your time, will change your life. I found reading one chapter a day and reflecting on it really helped me to connect more with my authentic self.

I love the examples of real events. They really helped me to feel understood and heard.

I highly recommend *FREEDOM to Be Me* and will definitely be reading this again.

Hayley Panton, BACPM DIP, Therapeutic Psychotherapist

There was little in this book that I didn't know, but much that I had forgotten. It is a brilliantly succinct distillation of Azmina's many years of learning from books, teachers and mentors and will save you having to read many other books!

Hearing things afresh in Azmina's words and from her perspective has helped some of the reminders I needed to stick. I particularly liked the chapter on listening to your intuition; the scientific facts and figures are fascinating and I am still working on noticing which of the three ways my intuition comes to me.

I love the way Azmina has given clear guidance as to how to use the information and tools she gives, and the questions at the end of each chapter really help to apply the learning. The book is easy to read as Azmina draws the reader in with her very frank and honest personal examples. She uses her own journey to illustrate the points she makes and explains how she changed from the fearful tongue-tied girl who arrived in England all alone at the age of 17, to the success she is today.

Diana Jordan, Divorce Consultant

Contents

Foreword

Dr Susan Jeffers and Azmina signing the licence agreement.

*A*zmina Jiwa was one of the very first licensed trainers of the Feel The Fear… And Do It Anyway® Training System, which was based on the bestselling book written by my late wife, Susan Jeffers, Ph.D.

Azmina has written a beautiful book, and she should be very proud of it. I know Susan would have been very proud of her in having the perseverance to write such a moving and inspirational book. Like her, she had the courage to go out there and share her intimate life experiences to encourage others to empower themselves to a better life.

Fear is natural, and everyone faces fear, but it can also be paralysing and can stop us from living the life we desire. This in many cases leads to anxiety and depression, which seem to be on the rise. That's why I'm pleased that Azmina has used what she has learned from Susan to support and empower more people through her workshops, one-to-one coaching, as a speaker, and now in this book.

In Azmina's book you'll find some much-needed tools and very relevant stories to help you to find happiness, fulfilment and peace. Her own life story is inspirational and a manifestation of how we can all transform ourselves to live a better, more loving and caring life.

Enjoy the book and, most importantly, do something with what you learn.

Mark Shelmerdine
CEO, Susan Jeffers, LLC

Acknowledgements

I know many writers will resonate with me when I say that there have many times when I've asked the questions: 'Why am I bothering to write?', 'Who am I to write a book?' and 'I feel like a fraud; I don't have my life completely sorted and I am guiding others'. With these voices in our head it is easy to give up.

We all need support, encouragement and gentle reminders when we embark on a project like writing a book, especially one's first book and a personal one at that.

I would like to thank:

Salim Jiwa, my husband, for his huge support and encouragement, for the holidays on the beach, and allowing me the space to write.

Jazzmin and Shamir, my son and daughter, for having faith in me.

Al Murtaza, my son-in-law, for always being so willing to give technical support.

Justyna, my daughter-in-law, for being so open and for her feedback.

Azmina Jiwa, myself, for having the courage to step up.

Shogufa Malekyar for encouraging and reminding me to start writing my book.

Nazmina Ladhani for gentle reminders to finish writing my book.

Lauren Gezurian, my sister-in-law, for her encouragement, support and feedback, and helping me to edit my story and photos.

Shelina Jaffer for feedback, encouragement and help with editing.

Maxine King, Sophia Jarrat and Shahenaz Lalani, my lovely friends, for their feedback.

Samantha Wade, my client, for her very constructive feedback.

Karen Williams, Librotas Book Mentor and author, for realigning me with my 'why' for writing this book, for planning the book and keeping me on track with patience and gentleness.

Sheryl Andrews, The Strength and Solution Detective and author, for clarity and confidence coaching to help me with my motivation and the realization that to work at my best I need deadlines. And for much-needed developmental editing.

Sam Pearce from SWATT Books for amazing creative book cover designs for the book and the internal typesetting.

Louise Lubke Cuss from Wordblink for editing and proofreading and supporting me to source the references.

And all my other friends who have been there for me. I thank you all.

Introduction

*A*s you have picked this book, I am guessing that you have reached a point in your life where you are ready for change and not happy with how you are living your life right now.

It may be that, like many, you have put the needs of others before yourself. Then you find yourself ending up at the bottom of the list, if you're on a list at all.

Perhaps you're going through a change in life and you've lost sight of who you are and what you want.

You may feel exhausted, worthless and anxious. You may spend much of your time crying, wondering how you are going to get to that place where you will feel happy again. Maybe you don't even remember a time when you were happy or what happiness is, but you do know that you want to be happy and free to be yourself.

I want you to know that there is light at the end of the tunnel. If I was able to do it, then so can you.

I am Azmina and I felt like that too. I remember the day that I was on my knees; I was sobbing and praying to God that somebody could give me the answer. I had read books, but it wasn't enough. Deep inside me, I knew that only I could make the changes I needed to make, but I didn't know how. Then something changed. Welcome to *FREEDOM to Be Me*. This is my story of how I transformed my unhappiness into happiness and gave myself the freedom to live the life I wanted to live.

And you can do the same.

What is happiness?

In my early years, I was essentially existing from day to day in fear, oblivious of the fact that I could be liberated from it. If you had asked me this question when I was in my forties, I could have only told you what unhappiness was: a sense of feeling unworthy, unfulfilled and with constant exhaustion, trying to please others to avoid rejection.

Now I know that happiness for me is a sense of feeling valuable, fulfilled, energized and no longer worrying if people like me. This is different to not caring what others think, as I still care about and value the opinions of others. Now I am not afraid to hear their opinions because I can now recognize it as a different perspective rather than a rejection of who I am and what I feel.

It is so good to finally be truly living and not just existing.

My journey of self-discovery started in 2002 whilst I was going through 'the change'. By this point I had lost a sense of who I was, and needed some clarity. This was when I attended my first personal developmental workshop, which made me connect with my younger self, that I just didn't recognize. This was life changing for me, as I met my inner child that had been neglected for all these years.

I realized that it was time to face my fears and release my true self. This led to a number of discoveries about myself that encouraged me to be more curious about how I could be more empowered and free to be me.

I instantly started to feel different inside. I noticed a small ball of energy in the centre of my gut that started to grow, which I nurtured. I decided that it was time to be kind and gentle to myself so that I could be me. This process took courage and determination, to allow me to let down my barriers, so that I could rid myself of my fears.

At last I had a sense of how I could be happy with myself and my life, and started to accept who I am and that I am worthy.

This resulted in my behaviour changing and had a massive impact on my life as a whole. My confidence grew, my relationships improved, and I was able to engage with people without fear of judgment. I still can't believe that I now have the confidence to speak in front of a large audience and yet previously it was difficult for me to even talk to a small group of three.

Having experienced the power of transformation, I went on to gain further knowledge and information through continued reading and workshops. Through this I became a personal development trainer and life coach. The lessons that I had learnt during my journey were so powerful for me, that I kept asking the question, Why isn't this more accessible? Hence the overwhelming desire to write this book, which contains my story and tools that you may find useful.

I am still learning about myself. The journey to self-discovery is a continuous one, often with challenges as we go along. I have learnt to apply my tools to re-centre myself when I realize that I am off course. This allows me to go deeper into myself to identify with feeling or fears that are holding me back from speaking my truth as it is today.

Now happiness for me is like this massive energy ball that radiates from inside me, deep down in my gut. I now feel able to give back to others without exhausting myself or depleting my own energy levels.

This book is an accumulation of 15 years of learning, and it is my hope and aspiration that by bringing all the principles, tools and techniques together in one book, you can also find yourself, like I did. It's all about 'the freedom to be me'!

Who is this book for?

If you are ready to find your true self, then this book is for you! Life comes with a number of different challenges – financial, mental, psychological, which can make us lose our way. Lose ourselves. Our inner voice is our true guide. If you feel you have lost your way, and would like a helping hand, this book is for you.

Whilst I was in my forties, you might be any age. But what is likely is that right now you are feeling very down, unhappy, worthless, tearful, exhausted, and anxious. You may even have physical symptoms like palpitations or feeling lethargic. Maybe your children have flown the nest, and you are left wondering who you are, what do you want to do with your life, and feeling unfulfilled.

You might feel that you cannot lift yourself out of those feelings that weigh so heavily on your heart right now.

You may find it hard to talk about how you feel because on the outside to others you appear to have no reason to complain. You have all you need. Some people may say you have all the material comforts, no financial pressures, nothing to be unhappy about, and yet you are still unhappy. If you are like me I would wake many mornings with heart palpitations, for which I had to take some medication because my heart felt like it was going to burst. I sometimes felt there was no point to life and a few times I remember crying really hard and asking God for help. I did not want to feel this way anymore.

You probably want to understand why you are feeling this way and like me you might have visited your doctor, had a blood test and maybe you now know you are peri menopausal, if not menopausal, and like me they might have given you some medication to help with depression or anxiety.

And despite this intervention things are still not right. At a deeper level you also sense there is more to these emotional highs and lows and you want answers. You are sick of simply existing and you want to truly live.

How to use this book

First I will be sharing the scientific basis of change. I will explore the principles of how our brain works and how our thoughts create experiences through thought, with the Law of Attraction. These principles helped me make sense of why I was feeling the way I was and why the techniques that I will share with you work.

You can use this book as a step-by-step process, working through one chapter at a time in order, which I recommend especially if you are very new to looking at yourself and only just starting to discover what you might need to feel free to be you.

For those more familiar with self-exploration and personal development, you can dip in and out and read the chapters that are relevant and resonate with you.

At the end of each chapter you will find a personal reflection section, which will invite you to delve deeper into the principles and allow you to apply them to your own circumstances. It is vital to recognize that the catalyst for change is the application of information and knowledge that you may gain from this book. The personal reflections are designed specifically for this purpose.

'The key to changing the world, to changing your life and empowering those around you is authenticity — the willingness to be yourself — the willingness to be vulnerable — the willingness to feel — the willingness to live. I am simply reminding you of who you truly are, supporting you into self-love and acceptance by eradicating the judgement that you have imposed on yourself and society has imposed on you.'

– Panache Desai

Reflection

How are you feeling at this moment in your life?

> With 0 being you are really feeling unhappy, down, not good enough, anxious etc and 10 being you are happy.
> Where are you today?

0 ⊢────────────────────────────────⊣ 10

Refer to this periodically and ask the question 'How do I feel?' to see visually what shifts you are making as you use the tools offered in the book.

Principles

There are some basic principles that made a significant difference to me, which I would like to share with you. These are the scientific principles of change: the **conscious and subconscious mind**, and the power of thought; the **Reticular Activity System** (RAS) which explores the filtration of information through the brain; and finally the **Law of Attraction**.

These principles allowed me to anchor my understanding of change by grasping the 'how' and 'why' of change.

How our brain works

The conscious and subconscious mind

> 'Use the power of your conscious
> and subconscious mind to create a
> vibrational match for the abundance
> you desire and deserve.'
>
> – Jack Canfield

When I came across this model and explanation of how my brain was working it made sense and helped me understand why certain things were happening and it put me back in control of my life. I remember sitting in a workshop with a picture of an iceberg as the trainer explained that only the top one eighth percent of the iceberg is visible, which represents the conscious

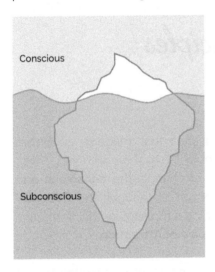

mind. The large bulk of the iceberg is submerged under water, representing the subconscious mind.

The conscious mind is our external experiences through our senses, that are present in our current awareness. Through the conscious mind, we gain self-awareness within the moment, both of our external and internal environments.

The subconscious mind on the other hand is the collection of memories and experiences, which can be retrieved as needed. We often draw upon habits through the subconscious mind in our daily lives. This would include basic activities such as social interaction, riding a bike or even driving a car.

When driving a car, for instance, once we have learnt to drive, we often find that the process becomes 'automatic'. We may not realize how often we look into our mirrors or use our indicators. We just do it. This is because our subconscious mind takes over the learned habits of driving. And often we don't need to revisit certain habits unless circumstances dictate otherwise. For instance if we travel abroad and cars are not left-hand driven, we will need to consciously relearn habits to ensure safety, until they too are embedded in the subconscious.

Changes therefore can be made by tapping into our memory bank within the subconscious mind, to adapt to different situations. This can be particularly relevant to behaviour and habits that may be holding us back from living the life we deserve.

For instance, when you have a thought like 'I can't deliver this project on time' this thought is often based on a belief system from past experience, stored in your subconscious mind. These thoughts and beliefs may have been relevant to an earlier stage in our life, but may no longer be helpful. However, until we consciously recognize that this belief system is not in our best interest, it will continue to dictate our actions and behaviour.

This thought then becomes a command to the subconscious mind.

This is just like you as the computer operator and Google. When you type into Google the information you want, you will get all the information that is stored in the database. Similarly, the command from the conscious mind is answered by the subconscious mind from its current database.

If we go back to the example of 'I cannot deliver this project on time' then you will think of all the reasons why you cannot do it. Now if you were more positive, you could consider saying 'Yes – I can meet the targets!' The subconscious mind will let you know of all the ways in which this can be achieved by tapping into your database of resources and experiences.

Therefore learning to become more aware of automatic habits within the subconscious is a highly effective way to promote change within your life by taking control.

Reticular Activity System (RAS)

*'The only thing that's keeping you
from getting what you want is the
story you keep telling yourself.'*

– Tony Robbins

The Reticular Activity System, sometimes referred to as the RAS, is our filtering system. There is a vast amount of information around us via all our senses and without some kind of filter, it would not be able to cope. The RAS allows our brain to filter information based on our daily agenda or beliefs gained through lifelong experiences.

For instance, if you were looking to buy a bright yellow convertible Mini, just to be different, you would soon start to notice that it was not as unusual as you expected, as you started to become more aware of these cars around you. This is the RAS filtering in the yellow Mini convertibles as your new agenda.

This can be relevant to more important situations like job hunting. If you were looking for a job and you believed there were no jobs in this economic climate, then your attention would be drawn to the people not getting jobs and you might miss the advertisements in the newspaper, despite reading them. Conversely, if you changed your belief to 'There are plenty of jobs for those who really want to work', then you would notice more job vacancies.

This system is particularly relevant to the background of each individual, depending on your life experiences. For instance, if you believe you are not good enough then you are more likely to be focused on areas where you are not performing well, despite outstanding performance in other areas. And this could make you self-critical.

Awareness of this RAS can allow you to recognize how your belief or agenda can have an impact on your life. Therefore learning to change your thoughts and beliefs will enable the RAS to change your life to a more positive one.

Law of Attraction

'The law of attraction states that whatever you focus on, think about, read about, and talk about intensely, you are going to attract more of into your life. Everything you want is out there waiting for you to ask. Everything you want also wants you. But you have to take action to get it.'

– Jack Canfield

The Law of Attraction is, in essence, the law of vibration. You might know from physics that everything has a vibration. This includes human, non-human, seen and unseen.

What we often don't realize is that thoughts have vibrations too. Each thought has vibrational energy which in turn can attract similar thoughts, events or even people, when vibrations are matched. When in search of an answer, for instance, you can find that you are drawn to a particular book or person who may tell you exactly what you needed to hear. However this is more aligned when we have clarity of thought.

Based on this principle we attract more of what we are thinking. You must have had experiences, such as when you are thinking of someone and they phone you, or someone mentions them to you. When these incidents happen we tend to say it is a coincidence, but in fact it is a vibrational match, and hence the Law of Attraction took place.

The Law of Attraction does not discriminate between negative and positive thoughts. So if you are not manifesting the things you want in your life, you need to become aware of your thoughts and feelings.

As you read this book you will learn to be more aware of your thoughts, as it is often your thoughts that are attracting the life you have now; and that is something you can actively choose to change to start attracting a life of freedom to be you.

CHAPTER ONE

Freedom to think differently

'Once you replace the negative
thoughts with positive ones you will
start having positive results.'

– Willie Nelson

As I have mentioned briefly before, our childhood conditioning often creates our beliefs, which in turn create our thoughts, and our thoughts create our feelings and emotions. And all of this leads to our behaviours, which give us the life we have now. And our beliefs can also come from our current experiences and from those around us. We can be influenced by what others say to us and about us and how they treat us.

We often adopt the habits and behaviours of adults around us, assuming their way to be the right way. And of course, we also make our own interpretations of what we think others think or feel about us. Beliefs can also come from the society we live in, like our faith, our school and teachers, and many other experiences we have in life.

I also believe there are some characteristics we are born with, like being an extrasensory person, or being a person who loves supporting others, and many more.

As children we often want to explore so much more than we do as adults. Sometimes adults, due to their own beliefs, their conditioning and their fears, will stop children exploring or they may label them as being too loud, too quiet, very clumsy, always naughty or lazy. The more a person hears these labels the more they start to believe them. Then we can become fearful, not only of physically exploring, but also of expressing ourselves.

Children with parents, teachers or other adults that encourage them, even when the child does not do as well as they had hoped, are more likely to develop into more positive adults. If our experiences are positive, we are more likely to grow up much more confident and feeling good about ourselves.

When a person is criticized often, then they are likely to develop a form of belief that they are not good enough and that may lead to low self-esteem. And sometimes we don't get criticized externally; we simply question ourselves when we don't seem to be the same as others. Comparing our internal world with the external world is one way of learning and making sense of how we belong, and many make the mistake of assuming that we have to be the same to fit it, whereas it can also be our differences that connect us.

Let me give you an example from my past. I remember my mother often asking me to be quiet, to avoid making my dad angry because he invariably lost his temper and would hit one of us children, usually my sister because she would speak out and oppose him.

As an adult my belief became that I had to be quiet when there were other people around. My thoughts were that people would get angry if I made a noise and they would not like me.

The emotions and feelings I experienced were fear. This showed up as behaviour where I was not doing what I wanted to do; I was putting pressure on myself to be really careful not to make any noise. I stayed out of the way even if it was not convenient to me. I became a people pleaser, thinking other people would say what a nice person I was. This meant that I was not getting my own needs met, and I didn't get to do what I wanted to do when I wanted to do it.

The wake-up call came when I noticed that I had passed that very same belief on to my own children. What was my parents' view had become my belief. I grew up not wanting to express my feelings and thoughts, and felt my ideas were not important.

One of the beliefs I had was that children don't know what they want, and they have to be told what to do. This, I believe, made my children grow up feeling not valued, and that their opinion was not important. And of course, I was also role modelling and demonstrating how to be someone who didn't value themselves or give an opinion often, if at all.

The knowledge that by changing my thoughts I can change how I feel gave me the freedom to choose how I want to feel, and you can do the same.

Like me you are probably more aware of your feelings than your thoughts. You may be feeling anxious, worried, unhappy, angry, frustrated, rejected, guilty, or hurt. These feelings are not created by other people or by the circumstances around you. They are there because of how you are thinking or perceiving the people or the circumstances. This I believe is a very important concept to understand and to remember. Other people and circumstances trigger our feelings that are already there; they do not create our feelings. I like the analogy Dr Wayne Dyer, who sadly is no longer with us, used in his talks, where he asked 'What do you get when you squeeze an orange – you are not going to get apple juice, you only get orange juice, which is what is inside'.

When you can acknowledge and accept these feelings, then you can stop letting them rule your life. When you acknowledge your feelings, then the feelings somehow dissolve or transform. Emotions are a form of energy. The Latin derivative for the word emotion, *emotere*, literally means **energy in motion**. Understanding **emotions are energy** implies that they are fluid, moving resources meant to be felt and released rather than suppressed and ignored.

Sometimes accepting your feelings may be difficult. What can help is to journal your thoughts. Often we try to push our feelings aside because we don't want to feel those feelings; they are too painful or we worry about what others think. So we get busy instead but the feelings don't go away. This only pushes our feelings deeper into us, and they keep coming up at different times in our lives. It can help to write them all out on paper, or you could talk to someone who is a good listener or to a therapist. I found personally that journalling didn't work and I really needed a non-judgmental listener. When you can acknowledge and accept your feelings in whichever way works for you then they will stop going around and around in your head.

Once you have accepted the way you are feeling, you will feel calmer and more in control because all that chatter that is going on inside now can stop and it creates space for a sense of calmness. From this place you can start to look within to what beliefs and thoughts are causing your feelings that are not keeping you feeling happy.

And if you choose to ignore this and you don't stop and reflect on what you are thinking and feeling then it is very likely that nothing will change and you will stay feeling stuck and unhappy.

Benefits of thinking differently

> You are able to change your emotional state that does not serve you at that moment.
> You will be able to change habits that are pulling you down in life.
> You will feel happier, as you have a choice on how you respond to what you cannot control.
> You will be able to create the life you want to live.
> You will have control over your inner state of being.

How to think differently

All our thoughts that we keep repeating are affirmations. When I was training to be a coach I was told that scientists believe that we have 65,000–75,000 thoughts a day and most of these are repeating thoughts, and many are negative thoughts that are no longer serving us. Whilst I have no idea how they prove this, I can tell you from my personal experience this feels about right. Therefore, becoming aware of your thoughts is the first step to change.

Once you recognize your beliefs and thoughts, then you can challenge them, if they are not serving you in a positive way.

The way you challenge them is by asking questions like:

> Is this thought true?
> Where did it come from?

It may be what your parents believed or something you have experienced. If you cannot find where they originated from, it's okay. You can still choose to think differently. The new thought you choose will be a positive affirmation of what you want.

All our thoughts that we keep telling ourselves, consciously or unconsciously, are affirmations. In this process what I am asking you to do is to become conscious of the thoughts that serve you and the thoughts that don't. And once you have identified those that don't serve you, then change them to a more positive thought.

One of the feelings I always had, when I was at a social gathering, was the feeling of not being confident. The thought behind this feeling was that 'I am not good enough'. As a result I did not talk much. I felt lonely and conscious of myself, and did not know what to say. My mind was full of thoughts like 'I do not want to say anything stupid'. My mind was cluttered with these thoughts, so I was not listening to what other people were saying and I could not think of anything that I could ask them. When I came home I felt even worse because I thought people must have thought I was stupid because I did not speak.

I started to challenge this thought 'I am not good enough'. I asked myself 'Is it really true?' and in reality, it is not true. Everyone has things they do well and other things they don't. So my new thought, or positive affirmation, was that 'We are all different, we all have our own unique gifts, so I am as good as and equal to other people'.

Whenever I found myself feeling like I lacked confidence, I would remind myself 'I am different and equal to everyone else'. After about a couple of months I found myself relaxing more, asking questions, and contributing if I wanted to, or just listening.

Positive affirmations

When we have a thought, or we say something out loud or we write it down, we are affirming to ourselves and others our current thinking and beliefs.

Once we become aware of our negative thoughts we then have the choice and the power to change them to positive. This is often referred to as creating a positive affirmation. It is recommended that the new affirmations be positive, e.g. what you want as opposed to what you don't want, so instead of saying 'I am not going to feel guilty', you would say something like 'I forgive myself, as it was the only way I knew at that moment'. They need to be in the present tense, so it would be 'I am now' not 'I will', otherwise the change you want will remain in the future. And they need to be personal to you as you can only change your own thoughts, not make others change theirs. Your positive energy can have an effect and influence others, but you cannot change others. So, if you initially wanted to say, 'My husband is thinking positively now' you would need to consider a positive affirmation that related to you personally like 'I am communicating positively today to get the best results from our relationship'.

And at all times, ensure your affirmations are believable to you. For example, if you are saying out loud 'I am confident' and there is a little voice that says 'No you are not' then a more believable affirmation might be 'I am working towards being more confident'.

Once you become aware of your thoughts, you then have the choice and the power to change them to more resourceful and empowering ones.

I suggest you repeat that thought several times a day. You can write them on Post-it notes and place them where you will be reminded of your affirmations, until they become a way of life. There is some evidence that it can take a minimum of 21 days to create new pathways in the brain but in my experience, we are all different, so it might take you less or more time, but it is important that you maintain the discipline until the new thought is habitual.

Once you work on one or two areas where you are not feeling happy, you will notice the change in you. Acknowledge and celebrate the change. This will keep the energy moving to do more towards living a happier life.

'Keep your thoughts positive because
your thoughts become your words.
Keep your words positive because
your words become your behavior.
Keep your behavior positive because
your behavior becomes your habits.
Keep your habits positive because
your habits become your values.
Keep your values positive because
your values become your destiny.'

– Mahatma Gandhi

Reflection

What feelings and behaviours are not serving you?

_____

_____

_____

What beliefs might you have to create those feelings and behaviours?

_____

_____

_____

List any beliefs you have become aware of.

_____

_____

_____

Make a list of thoughts that you feel are not serving you as you become aware of them.

_____

_____

_____

If you are not aware of your thoughts, then make a list of your feelings that don't feel good. For example, if you are feeling exhausted, then your thought might be 'I am lazy if I don't get the task done', or 'I feel guilty because my husband is working so hard'. Simply be curious about what you hear yourself saying or thinking.

Now challenge that thought.

Is it really always true?

_____

Where did it come from?

_____

_____

_____

Who says that it is true?

_____

_____

_____

What would I be without that thought?

_____

_____

_____

What could be a different thought that sounds believable, is positive, present tense and about you?

_____

_____

_____

Write this on a few cards or sticky notes or whatever works to remind you of this new thought.

When you notice any changes in your feelings and your behaviours, acknowledge them and celebrate in a way that feels right for you.

CHAPTER TWO

Freedom to accept yourself

'To accept ourselves as we are
means to value our imperfections
as much as our perfections.'

– Sandra Bierig

Self-acceptance means to fully accept the person you are right now in this moment. All that you like about yourself and all that you don't like about yourself, the things you criticize yourself for and all your feelings and emotions, positive or negative.

Which means that you recognize your value as a person, that is your self-worth, for being here in the world. Being happy being the person you are regardless of your faults or weaknesses.

Acceptance also means to accept the circumstances you find yourself in at any time, whether it is due to you having made a wrong decision, where instead of feeling guilty you forgive yourself, or when life happens and you have no choice, for example losing your job, you accept the reality of this and focus on the next steps to finding another job.

You don't have to like or enjoy everything you accept; it just means that you are acknowledging the reality as it is now. When we resist what is present in this moment it will only persist.

There seems to be a belief that by accepting everything nothing will change, but in fact by accepting there is a greater chance of success and making the changes that we want. This is true because when we don't accept we are resisting what is the truth, in this moment. Once accepted and acknowledged, there is a shift in energy. The mind and body relaxes. This gives us space to create whatever we want next.

Each moment is creating the next moment, so when you resist, for example if you are not accepting something that you feel you did wrong and are feeling guilty about it, this thought and feeling in this moment will create the same in the next moment. You keep feeling guilty, your mind is cluttered and your body is not at ease. Now let's say you accept that whatever you did, in the past, is okay. You did what you thought was best at that time. You ask for forgiveness if that is needed or appropriate. You can now let go of the guilt. You feel relief. Your next moment is a happier one than the previous moment.

As babies we are born feeling so free and accepting of ourselves. Babies are just being themselves. They express themselves and their feelings, without any fear of judgment or inhibitions, and then they move on to the next moment. They live so much in the present.

What I have noticed is that generally most parents are always praising their babies and children for being able to stand, walk, say their first words or ride a bike.

At the same time when children express themselves by being just who they are or they are exploring their own abilities, or their environment, parents and adults generally start to inhibit them by saying 'don't' do this or that.

I remember one of my friends came over for coffee with her three-year-old, and the girl was having fun and she was making loud noises and happily playing. But her mum asked her to stop being so loud, and labelled her as always being too loud. If her daughter hears this often then she may grow up believing she is always too loud. She may live her life by being extra quiet, in fear that she will be judged for being herself, as I was. And others may purposefully be louder and ignore the impact it has on others.

When we start to attend school, our parents and we as children can start to compare ourselves with others. I remember telling my parents my exam marks; instead of any praise, I was asked why didn't I get full marks or why did that other child do better than you?

As teenagers some of us are told we could be slimmer or don't wear that dress; it shows your bottom too much. This was my thing and I was also imposing it on my daughter and making her conscious of her body, rather than loving her body just as it is.

My daughter is a highly sensitive being, but as a young child I did not accept her personality. She would feel everything very strongly. I labelled her sensitive and touchy because I thought she should not go into her feelings and she should just get on. She grew up feeling that something was wrong with her. Now I know better, I can do better, and so I really appreciate that this is her gift and she has been my greatest teacher to learn to accept and express my feelings.

As a parent, I am also aware that I was very strict with my children and I was stopping them expressing themselves because of my fear of others judging me as a mother who couldn't discipline her children. This resulted in my children not being very confident. I was particularly worried when my daughter, at the age of six, was not happy for me to leave her at one of her friends' birthday parties, and my son's school report said he did not speak up as much as he could.

Around this time I attended a parenting course where I learnt that our feel good factors, energy and motivation, come from being praised and not criticized. I made changes in how I was with my own children, and my daughter has told me that she actually remembers feeling differently when I changed my behaviour. I did not apply this learning to myself until many years later. Now I am willing and more able to give myself praise and receive it.

If we get enough reminders of our mistakes and how others interpret our behaviour, we can start to believe these labels. For example, a person sat on a sofa could be labelled as either lazy or relaxed; it is simply a perception. These labels can then become our identity. We start to feel that we are that label and often lose a sense of our self and who we really are. We then risk not accepting our true self just as we are today.

Somehow there is a belief in our society that to improve our behaviour and performance we need to be told where we are going wrong and often it does not include praising good behaviour and performance in equal measure. I believe that to get the best out of ourselves and each other we need to be willing to invest the time to discuss both equally, and the common belief is that it takes too long, and it is quicker to just talk about what needs to improve or what went wrong. In reality this actually slows progress and improvement down, because the individual has to work much harder at remembering what is going well to process and accept the criticism effectively.

It is no wonder then, as adults, that we have become our own worst critics. We are so hard on ourselves, so very judgmental, and comparing ourselves to others and feeling unhappy with who we are. How many times do you find yourself criticizing your body? Or criticizing what you did or did not do perfectly? How many times do you say things like 'That was stupid of me', 'I am not as good as others', 'I am too fat' or 'I never get it right'?

These thoughts are likely to generate a sense of being unworthy and not good enough and a lack of acceptance about yourself. What I have come to learn is that when we accept ourselves we have more energy and enthusiasm for life. This belief was strengthened by what I read in Dr Hawkins' book. In his book, *Power vs Force – The Hidden Determinants of Human Behavior,* David R. Hawkins, M.D., PhD writes

> *The critical response point in the scale of consciousness calibrates at level 200, which is the level associated with integrity and courage. All attitudes, thoughts, feelings, associations, entities, or historical figures below that level of calibration make a person go weak – those that calibrate higher make subjects go strong. This is the balance point between weak and strong attractors, between negative and positive influence*[1].

Dr Hawkins' Map of Consciousness[2] shows Guilt with a calibration of 30, Fear at 100, Acceptance at 350 and Love at 500.

My understanding from this is that when we do not accept ourselves and have feelings like guilt, fear and other negative feelings, we will feel a lack of energy. When we are more positive and accepting of ourselves we will have more energy and therefore be motivated to do more and feel happier.

Knowing this made sense of why I always felt tired and exhausted. I often felt guilty especially if something went wrong; I used to feel that it might have been my fault, that I had done something wrong.

By not accepting ourselves we risk suffering with low self-esteem and confidence, and we can become a people pleaser, because we are looking for praise from others to feel good about ourselves. Some people go on a shopping spree and others may binge on food to make themselves feel good. But this external affirmation doesn't last very long, so we are often on a continuous quest of doing what others want us to do.

When we have low self-esteem we might become withdrawn and shy or we might be over-expressing and overacting in order to get noticed.

By not accepting yourself, or the circumstances and situations presented to you, you can start to feel exhausted, unhappy, stuck, unfulfilled, and even depressed. It is a feeling of just existing rather than living life to the full. Your focus is generally on where you are not good enough, where you are not perfect. You are not seeing where you are great, all your gifts, the things that you are good at, and therefore you will not able to express your true potential.

Imagine if, instead of encouraging a child who is just beginning to walk, and is falling as they take a step, you tell the child off every time they fall because it was not perfect, how is this child ever going to learn to walk?

And it is never too late. As adults we are now the parent of our own self, our own inner child. It is really important that we learn to accept ourselves completely with what we perceive our faults to be, our qualities, strengths, weaknesses, failures and everything about ourselves.

When life happens, say yes!

When we accept the situation and circumstances we find ourselves in when things happen that are out of our control – be it a traffic jam, someone letting you down, illness, accident, losing your job, others not wanting a relationship with you and so on, then it is also important to apply the same process of acceptance.

Dr Susan Jeffers explains this really well. She says 'Say yes'. It is not about saying yes to everything and everyone but it is about accepting what is, rather than trying to pretend it is not happening or wishing it wasn't. Here is a passage from her book *Feel the Fear and Do It Anyway*[3]:

> The phrase 'say yes' means 'to agree to' those things that life hands to us. Saying yes means letting go of resistance and letting in the possibilities that our universe offers in new ways of seeing the world. It means to relax bodily and calmly survey the situation, thereby reducing upset and anxiety.
>
> Saying no creates tension, exhaustion, wasted expenditure of energy, emotional upheaval, or at worst it creates apathy. The truth of the matter is that saying yes is our only hope.
>
> Not only is saying yes our antidote to dealing with day-to-day disappointment, rejection, and missed opportunities [...] it is the miracle tool for dealing with our deepest, darkest fears.

I believe by saying yes we create more peace and flow. It wasn't easy, but when I learnt to accept myself and the circumstances I found myself in it was a repeated process of keeping changing my chatterbox, that is the thoughts running in my head, from criticism to acceptance.

Learning to accept your self is a process; it doesn't generally happen overnight but you can instantly feel hope and relief because you know you can and will be able to change how you think and feel with practice. This is not always easy to do, as we can be our own worst critics. This does require practice and it is a lifelong journey. For some of the things you may be able to use the process much quicker and at other times it could even take months or years.

What I noticed with me was that gradually over two to three weeks I began to have more energy, was more at peace and I was motivated to do more of what I wanted to do. As I applied this acceptance to more areas of my life, I started to value myself; my fear of judgment was reduced and I felt a lot happier.

I believe all things happen for a reason. Even if we cannot understand why straight away, I do believe it is for our spiritual growth, and to ensure we live our purpose. When we find ourselves in situations which we did not expect, it is an opportunity to ask questions like 'What is the learning here?' or 'What is the opportunity here?' This can often give us a clue as to what we need to learn or perhaps what opportunity this situation is presenting before us.

An example of acceptance is a cousin of my husband who had a tumour in his head. He lost his sight and speech and was paralysed from the hips down. He was, of course, angry and sad and had many other feelings during the grieving process, and then as he accepted his situation he was more calm and restful and that is when he decided he wanted to contribute in spite of what had happened and he wanted to find a purpose. He wasn't willing to be a vegetable in his house. He has since given many lectures, through his computer, on awareness of disabilities and how they need to be treated and he also teaches Braille to blind children.

This is a great example of when life happens to us and the only thing in our control is the way we think and respond to the situation.

From this example, I think we can see that there is a spiritual reason why things happen. We as human beings are not able to see this except with hindsight. Sometimes it may be to find our true purpose as in the example above; at other times it may be that we need to take care of ourselves more than we are doing. I know of a friend who recovered after suffering a heart attack. He accepted what happened to him rather than focusing on 'why me' and resisting. He changed his priorities from focusing on work all the time to having a more balanced life.

How to accept yourself

There are four steps to the acceptance process.

> Aware
> Acknowledge
> Accept
> Set a new intention

Aware

It always begins with becoming aware this isn't what we want in our lives. Aware of the thoughts running in your head. Aware of circumstances not in your control. Becoming aware, I think, is half way towards change happening.

Acknowledge

Next you acknowledge those thoughts and feelings, which are probably going round and round in your head, as well as the situation or circumstance that you are resisting. Become present to the now. You can do this by naming the feelings, or by focusing on your breathing, or just watching the feeling and creating peace with all that does not feel okay, as being perfect in this moment. You could simply have an affirmation; as Louise Hay, author of many bestselling self-help books, would say, 'It's all working perfectly for my higher good'.

Accept

Once you acknowledge and accept the feelings and/or the situation or circumstance, your mind can be at rest. The act of acceptance can allow the feelings to melt away and transform. Your body can relax and then the next layer is to accept that whatever situation or event you are facing, it is happening for a reason.

Set a new intention
From here you can make a choice of what you want to change. How would you like to feel? What thoughts and beliefs need to change? You can visualize, write new thoughts or affirmations using the affirmation process discussed in Chapter 1, Freedom to think differently, and the principle of the Law of Attraction from the Principles chapter.

Some changes are instant – it's those 'aha' moments we all have – and some changes are not instant, but slowly you will start to change and bring about more peace, happiness and fulfilment in your life.

When you don't accept yourself or your circumstances you stay stuck in the moment and nothing changes.

Benefits of acceptance

When you start to accept yourself and your circumstance you are able to:

> Listen to your intuition and your inner calling much more.
> Feel you are in the flow with life much more than before.
> Experience less fear of others judging you.
> Be more confident to say and do what you want in your life rather than trying to please others or get the approval of others.
> Have more energy, motivation and clarity of mind, because you will be living in the present moment rather than in the past or the future.

'Because one is content with oneself, one doesn't need others' approval. Because one accepts oneself, the whole accepts him or her.'

– Lao Tzu

Reflection

Make a list of:

Your strengths

_____

_____

Your positive qualities

_____

_____

Compliments people give you

_____

_____

Criticism you give yourself or hear from others

_____

_____

Now notice which ones you can accept and which you cannot.

Then decide which ones you want to change and which ones you want to learn how to embrace and accept as being you. Any behaviour that you don't like or accept as being you, consider what you would like to have happen instead. For example if someone says you are very quiet and you don't accept that, you can choose to be more vocal.

You could then make an affirmation. I particularly like these ones from one of Dawn Breslin's workshops[4], but feel free to make up your own. To know more about how to create positive affirmations please refer to Chapter 1, Freedom to think differently.

> Today I accept myself exactly as I am. I release the need to judge and criticize myself.
> I accept myself for all the positive qualities that reunite me with my soul and remind me how unique I actually am.
> I accept that I always do my best in each and every situation; this is all I ever do.
> I accept myself and no longer compare myself to others.
> I accept where my life is at and exactly who I am today. By nurturing myself, I will gently evolve into a stronger human being.

Make a list of what you have learnt from any past difficult or painful situations/circumstances that were not in your control.

_____

_____

_____

Notice and write down any person, situation or circumstances that you are resisting in the present moment, if any.

_____

_____

_____

Can you give yourself the permission to accept it for now? If you do, you are saying YES to life happening.

_____

_____

_____

What lessons or opportunities could this situation or circumstance potentially bring for you?

_____

_____

_____

Is there anything you can do about it?

_____

_____

_____

CHAPTER THREE

Freedom to take responsibility

'You relinquish your power when you
blame others for situations in your life.
The blame does not change the situation
and only keeps you in a victim mentality.
Accept that the situation occurred and
find a way to transcend it and you will
reclaim your power and become the victor.'

– Nanette Mathews

When I talk about taking responsibility I am not talking about your duties at work, or home. Of course, you may have certain responsibilities which need to be done day to day, things like keeping the house clean, for example, or the cooking, or doing paperwork. What I am talking about here is the responsibility for your own happiness and your sense of self-worth. You are the driver of your life. You are totally responsible for your life. This is one of the principles you need to embrace in order to have real freedom to be who you want to be, have what you want to have in your life, do what you want to do and most importantly feel how you want to feel.

We often feel that other people are responsible for us not feeling good about ourselves. We often say things like 'They put me down, my boss does not like me, they made me angry' etc. Or we think our circumstances are not right for us to be happy.

As I explained in Chapter 1, our emotions and feelings come from our own thoughts. Therefore, you can change your feelings by changing your thoughts. This is a choice; you can develop the ability to consciously decide to think and feel differently. Being human we cannot avoid feelings that are negative, but we can change the thoughts that generate the feelings and we are the only person that can be, and is, responsible for that change.

When we fail to take responsibility it is more likely that we will stay stuck, blaming others or our situation, leaving ourselves feeling helpless, powerless and often alone.

If you want a promotion, if you want acknowledgement, if you want to feel valued, if you want a more fulfilling life, then it is your responsibility to make the change to make these things happen in your life.

In my workshops I ask the participants what makes them happy, and what makes them unhappy, and the kind of list I get is:

> Children
> Money
> Other people
> Health
> Work

These are all things outside of us. It is very occasionally that someone will say that their happiness is from within them.

The simple fact is your happiness does not depend on these outside factors; it actually depends on how you think about the situations and how you react to them. You cannot always change your circumstances and you cannot change other people, but what you can change is your response to them.

In my talks I often ask the participants what would be their thoughts and feelings if at a social event, for example, a friend were to walk past them without saying 'Hello' or acknowledging them in some way.

The responses were as follows:

> I feel that she thinks too much of herself.
> I feel hurt.
> I think I may done something wrong.
> I think she might have something on her mind.
> I think she was in a hurry.

As you can see, everyone has very different thoughts about what the behaviour means and therefore how they feel is not because of this person who passes them by without acknowledging them, but their own interpretation and perception based on their life experiences and beliefs.

The responsibility of how we feel therefore is in our control. And if your current thinking is not generating feelings that serve you then you can choose to change the thoughts. The truth is that we will only really know the true meaning of their behaviour if we actually ask the other person what was happening for them.

I know this is really hard to get your head around at first, because it really does feel like it is out of our control, but trust me. When you take responsibility you give yourself the freedom to be you.

When you blame other people or your circumstances then you are giving up your own power to change. You are in effect saying others are responsible and then nothing changes in your life. You have no power to have the life you want. You then begin to feel like a victim of other people and your circumstances.

The victim mentality means you are blaming your circumstances and other people for your feelings and your situation. You may be saying 'If only they would change how they treat me then I will be fine', 'I am frustrated because...', 'I am angry that they...', 'They have upset me', 'I am disappointed with...' and so on. Or you may be thinking you are not happy because you don't live in the right area or you may be blaming the job market for not having a job, etc.

Let's look at some areas of your life where you may be giving up your power to feel worthy, valued, happy and fulfilled.

At work

Perhaps you are not getting a pay rise or a promotion and you are blaming your boss or colleagues. Maybe you are blaming the job market for not getting a job. Or perhaps you don't like your work, but are too afraid to lose the security it provides.

At work you may be unhappy because others are getting promoted and you are not. What are your choices if you were fully responsible for where you want to be in life?

If you are responsible then you might:

> Consider if you do actually need to put more effort into what you are doing.
> Voice what you want.
> Be more assertive when you are communicating with your boss. (Many of us seem to believe that others should

know what we want, or that they can see that this is what we want.)
> Leave the job.
> Find out what the company needs from you in order to be promoted.

Before attending one of my workshops I like to get to know what challenges my clients are facing and what they want to get out of the workshop.

I remember one particular client was not getting on with her boss. After the workshop she said things had changed, and their relationship had really improved. This is because she took responsibility for how she was feeling about him; she no longer blamed him for making her feel that way, and she was able to be more upfront and assertive. That way the boss knew what she wanted, which meant their communication was better and she was happy.

In relationships

Maybe you are blaming your ex-husband, husband, partner, family members or friends for being the cause of your unhappiness, hurt, anger, tiredness, for not doing what you want to do, for not behaving how you want them to behave.

If you are responsible then:

> Maybe you need to communicate clearly and positively what you want.
> Maybe you have to accept others for who they are.
> Maybe you have to learn to say no.

I had a friend who used to complain about her teenage son making her miserable. I wanted to know how he did that and she said he ignored her and her friends when he came home. He just rushed upstairs without greeting her and her friends.

She was blaming her son for making her miserable, because she was interpreting the behaviour of going upstairs as ignoring. It also turned out that she worried that her friends would judge her as a bad mother. This preyed on her mind and made her unhappy. She did not realize that she was responsible for her fears of feeling judged; it was not her son making her miserable.

I too was blaming my husband for not allowing me to go out when he was home. I was blaming him for not letting me do what I wanted to do to enjoy myself. When he first questioned me about going out when he was at home or for being out when he came home, I began to think that he did not want me to be out; he was not allowing me to go out. I believed it was his fault that I was not doing things I enjoyed doing.

Learning that I am responsible for what I want to do in my life put the power of change in my hands. So then I asked myself, what did I need to do to have the life I want? I needed to communicate my needs and what I wanted to my husband.

I needed to communicate in an assertive way, which meant saying what I wanted, and how I felt, rather than accusing him of not letting me go out when he was at home. For me I would need to say 'I really want to go, and I understand how you feel, and I will be out for a couple of hours.' I talk more about how to communicate your feelings assertively in Chapter 8, Freedom to speak your truth.

When we communicate our needs by expressing what we want and what we feel then the other person does not feel under attack and is less likely to get defensive and on the contrary, if he or she loves you, they will want you to be happy. Therefore they will try to understand and even help you.

In my case, after I found the strength to speak to my husband and express what it was that I wanted, I realized that the only reason why he did not like being alone at home was his own insecurities from his own childhood experiences. It did not have anything to do with him trying to control me. In fact my husband did love me and wanted me to be happy. Having an honest conversation about my feelings allowed him to deal with his feelings. Sometimes we allow others to grow when we don't try to do everything to please them.

When I realized that I was afraid of rejection and that is why I was doing what my husband wanted rather than what I wanted, then I had choices: to stay in this unhappy state, face my fear and communicate my needs, be more assertive, or to leave.

I chose to communicate and be assertive. As my husband truly loved me, and I was able to communicate without blaming, I am now living the life I love. I go out with friends, I go on retreats, I volunteer, as well as doing things we love to do together, like hiking and travelling.

On the other hand I know someone who was in a similar situation, and did the same thing as me, but her husband was not willing to let go, so she chose to leave the marriage. It was tough at first, but she said she was so much happier in spite of having lots of challenges.

Recently one of my relatives has felt hurt because I had not fulfilled her expectations of how I should be behaving, and therefore she has chosen not to talk to me. Here I have a choice to feel bad about the situation or to feel peace. I understand that I am the one who is responsible for my own feelings, regardless of the behaviour of others. I have chosen to be at peace with her behaviour.

It is important to understand that in any given moment each one of us can only behave the way we know how, with the knowledge, the feelings we are feeling and our energy at that moment. What is the point of blaming that person, because in that moment, that's the only way they know how to behave? You don't need to blame yourself either. This will allow you to be more forgiving to others and yourself.

So taking responsibility means not to blame others for what you have, for what you are doing or feeling. Instead ask yourself 'What can I do about this feeling or situation, if I am wholly responsible for it?' Once the power is in your hands then you are not reactive; you have choices on how you behave. Instead of blame, you may have compassion for the person; you may want to say something to make them aware of their behaviour and how it is affecting you or you may just want to let go of what they did or said.

Often it is much easier to be a victim. At an unconscious level, it gives us a sense of security and safety; it is a place we know, a place that is familiar but it is not necessarily a happy place, or a place of growth, and it can become our comfort zone.

By staying in the victim mode and your comfort zone you don't have to face your fears: fear of rejection, failure, hurting others' feelings, not having enough money, losing your job, not fitting in with peers, wanting everyone to like you. You don't have to step out of your comfort zone and be blamed for anything; you are safe from criticism and judgment.

Of course once you start to take responsibility, you may displease some people. You will have to start saying no. You will have to be honest and speak your mind, your truth. You might start to feel guilty. These are all the feelings you will have to face and deal with.

It is a process; with awareness, taking baby steps, and becoming more confident, you will start to feel good about yourself. You will start doing what you want to do. Gradually it gets easier and easier. Be kind and gentle with yourself in the process.

Without stepping out of the comfort zone, we do not grow. We continue to feel unhappy and we do not feel fulfilled, which means we stop growing and growth is one of our basic needs.

According to Maslow's hierarchy of needs (1943)[5], we will continually be motivated to grow to meet our needs, from the basic needs of food, shelter, and security to self-fulfilment. Unfortunately, this natural growth process can be interrupted by our childhood conditioning and past experiences. According to Maslow only one in a hundred people become fully self-actualized which I interpret to mean that only one in a hundred people will fully have the freedom to be themselves and be on purpose. It is my hope that this book and many other teachings will ensure that this number grows in time. Everyone deserves to know they matter and they are of value and should be free to be themselves.

Anthony Robbins, a renowned coach and speaker, says that success and happiness can be found by meeting six core needs[6]. These are the need to have certainty, variety, significance, love and connection, growth and contribution. Each day we fulfil these needs either in a resourceful way or a non-resourceful way. One example of meeting your needs in a non-resourceful way is blaming and being a victim.

I do believe and have experienced that happiness and fulfilment come by stepping out of our comfort zone. As you can see from my story, writing this book is another huge step towards my own freedom to be me.

By not taking responsibility for your own happiness you stay a victim. You keep blaming others. You feel powerless.

What are the benefits of taking responsibility?

> Taking responsibility gives you the power to steer your life how and where you want.
> You have greater choices in how you want to feel, and what you want to have or be in your life.
> You can achieve your own goals and dreams much more confidently.
> You will feel happier and be more fulfilled.

How to take responsibility and step out of your comfort zone

1. Become aware of when and where you are blaming someone or blaming your circumstances.
2. Take responsibility for what you are feeling, having, and doing.
3. Ask yourself what you want.
4. Ask what is stopping you.
5. Set yourself some small goals to overcome whatever is stopping you.

Once you identify the reason why you are not taking responsibility then it is easier to work out the steps you need to take. By taking responsibility for your own life you will live a life that you want for yourself. A life of happiness, peace and freedom.

'The greatest day in your life and mine is when we take total responsibility for our attitudes. That's the day we truly grow up.'

– John C. Maxwell

Reflection

Notice where you are blaming, getting upset, frustrated, feeling helpless, self-pitying etc.

What benefits, security, or safety are you deriving from this?

_____

_____

_____

What action can you take to step out of that comfort zone?

_____

_____

_____

CHAPTER FOUR

Freedom to be grateful

'Gratitude always comes into play;
research shows that people are happier
if they are grateful for the positive
things in their lives, rather than worrying
about what might be missing.'

– Dan Buettner

eing grateful and offering gratitude is universal and practised freely by everyone in the world. It is about showing appreciation when someone has helped us or served us and it is appreciation of something we value.

I think most of us have taken gratitude for granted. Saying thank you is something we are taught from a very young age. As children our parents, aunts, uncles and grandparents try really hard to teach us these manners of saying thank you whenever someone gives us something or does something for us.

I remember as a child I used to say things like 'God thank you for Mummy and Daddy, thank you for the food we eat etc'. It was rote learning, like learning times tables in maths.

As grown-ups saying thank you becomes a habit, on shopping trips, at the workplace, in the street, just part of everyday life. And then there are times when we express genuine thanks with passion, because we really appreciate someone's help.

Most religions have prayers of gratitude. Religions teach us to be grateful for everything we have in our life.

In Christianity
Rejoice always, pray constantly. Give thanks for all circumstances, for this is the will of God towards you in Christ Jesus.
Thessalonians 5:16-18 NIV

In Islam
If you give thanks I will give you more. Qur'an 14:7

In Judaism
O Lord my God, I will give thanks to you forever. Psalms 30:20

I wonder how many of us who recite the prayers of gratitude as part of our faith are chanting and reciting like a parrot without knowing why.

One of the reasons why we are feeling worthless, unhappy, anxious, and depressed is because we get caught up with what is not working in our lives. We focus on what we don't have, and things that are not going according to how we want them to be. We worry about what we are not good at. We compare ourselves to others, and feel we are not good enough or we don't have enough.

Some of us are not happy because we don't have the right partner in our life, or the house we want, or the job, or anything else, so we feel we are not good enough. We criticize ourselves for not being perfect, or, when we get one negative comment from someone, we have a tendency to focus on that one comment and we do not take notice of four other positive ones we may have received. If there is one criticism at work, we start to feel bad all day. It's like noticing one black dot on a white cloth.

If the prayers of gratitude are recited by focusing on what we have and not on what we don't have, our feelings of unhappiness and feeling down are lifted. My experience of doing a gratitude journal came after the first workshop I attended, where I learnt about gratitude and was given a gratitude journal. At first I could not think of many things to write and felt silly if I wrote about the obvious things like having enough food, and a roof over my head. As days went by I became aware of many more things I have in my life. My appreciation of little things also grew and I remember feeling so much happier as a result of this.

By not practising gratitude you miss out on the abundance that you already have and being able to attract more of what you want.

The benefits of gratitude

Life is not perfect and every day will not be perfect, and yet an attitude of gratitude helps to:

> Change the focus from negative to positive which gives us a new perspective of self and others.
> Put things into perspective during difficult times. When we offer gratitude, it is an act of appreciation, an act of humility.
> Show us the abundance of life. Whatever we focus on is what we attract more of in our life and this in turn makes us feel content, joyful, loving and happy.

> Appreciate our own greatness, our uniqueness. When we are grateful for all the qualities and gifts we have, that helps us focus on our strengths and the things we do well, which encourages us to do more of what we love, which means we serve and support more people and make a bigger difference in our world. And by doing this we have more compassion for the weaknesses in ourselves and others.

> Feel a higher sense of self-worth, because being grateful takes us away from the 'poor me' state to noticing the things we do have. This takes away fear which in turn will make us feel more alive, positive, and happy.

> Reduce depression, because when we focus on what we have we reduce fear, worry and concern which in turn changes the chemical imbalance in our system, which leads to more joy and happiness in our life.

> Take us out of our ego, our small world, into the universality and expansion of our existence.

> Offer gratitude for something that feels painful which supports us to value the growth and the learning that comes from it much more quickly. My belief is that many things that happen to us in our life are for a reason: to learn and grow. If we look at painful experiences as an opportunity for our growth towards a happier and more joyful life, then it is easier to offer gratitude. I am sure some of you will know of people who have had cancer, another serious illness or lost their job, and at a later date have said 'That was the best thing in my life'. These events help us to see what is really important in life. This helps us to give up our false fears and worry and really start to live life the way we want to.

> Improve our health. By living in the present moment our body is likely to relax which improves our immune system, improves blood pressure and we are very likely to sleep better.

> Stop us feeling resentful and envious of others, because being grateful makes us feel like our own plate is full and therefore we are more likely to be more forgiving, generous and compassionate.

And, like a muscle, this mental state can be strengthened with practice. There are many ways of practising gratitude.

How to practise gratitude

Journal
You can journal every night or morning or at any other time that suits you. When you start to write this journal every day, write about 10 things that you are grateful for. These may be things you have, things you did maybe the previous day, people you met or the things others did for you. It might be the way you were being, like positive or compassionate. I recommend that this becomes a lifelong habit that you do and you can do it until you notice that it is the norm to feel gratitude for everything in your life, even the things that are painful.

Post-it notes
Another way to remind yourself to feel and show gratitude is to have some Post-it notes saying '*I am so grateful for_____*'. Fill in the blanks with whatever one or two things that you feel a sense of gratitude for in your life. Put these notes in your car, on a mirror or fridge. These act as great reminders to trigger you to think differently.

Thank you notes
You can write thank you notes: whether in response to a gift or kind act, or simply as a show of gratitude for someone being in your life, getting into the habit of writing thank you letters can help you express gratitude in addition to simply feeling it inside. The act of writing can also help to embed the thought and make it more permanent.

Count your blessings

Once a week, reflect on events for which you are grateful, and write them down. As you do, feel the sensations of happiness and thankfulness you felt at the time they happened, going over them again in your mind. You can literally count your blessings by being consciously aware of just how much you are grateful for.

Prayer

Expressing thanks during your prayers is another way to cultivate gratitude. If you have a religious practice where you do a gratitude prayer using a rosary, you might be repeating the words of gratitude and moving the beads and the invitation is to really be conscious of what you are specifically grateful for with each bead of the rosary or chant. In my experience you can start to feel different inside and the little things you were worried about don't seem as important anymore. Again be kind to yourself; this is something to practise and develop.

'Gratitude makes sense of our past, brings peace for today, and creates a vision for tomorrow.'

– Melody Beattie

Reflection

Write 10 things that you are grateful for in this moment.

1. _____

2. _____

3. _____

4. _____

5. _____

6. _____

7. _____

8. _____

9. _____

10. _____

What painful event have you experienced in the past?

_____

_____

_____

_____

What lessons have you learnt from that experience?

_____

_____

_____

How will you keep up a regular practice of being grateful?

_____

_____

_____

CHAPTER FIVE

Freedom to be special and unique

'Fitting in allows you to blend in with everyone else, but being different allows you to be yourself, to be unique and to be more creative.'

– Sonya Parker

We are all born to be OUR special and unique self. It is our birthright. Just as we each have our own unique fingerprints, we also have our own unique purpose too. There is no one who looks exactly like you or me. This uniqueness is not only in human beings but in nature too. No two leaves or trees are the same.

I do believe that each one of us is born with our own special gifts and we are born to share and contribute these gifts to the world. We have a special purpose for being on this earth. Just like a huge jigsaw puzzle, where every piece is different, unique and special, each piece is very important to complete the picture. And like a jigsaw puzzle, sometimes it takes time to work out how each piece fits in and connects to the rest and yet we also know there is a place. Each one of us is also different, special, unique and very important.

Just like the jigsaw puzzle, where all the pieces connect with each other, if one piece in the puzzle changes then that affects all the other pieces around that particular piece. In the same way we also have connections with each other in that our thoughts, energy and actions have an impact on those around us. Our connections are there so we can serve one another. If we did not have farmers, salespeople in the shops, rubbish collectors, how would we survive? Each one of us is needed and we are all as important as every other person.

You are unique, because no one will have experienced life exactly as you have. In other words, no one has walked in your shoes. Not even siblings from the same family. As we go through the journey of our life, at any given point in our life we are the product of our beliefs and experiences and these will be different for all of us.

Why do some of us not feel unique and special?

I believe that when we are growing up, if we are repeatedly told or made to feel we are unique, special and as important as anyone else, we will focus our attention on what is special and unique about us and see it as a gift. Whereas if we are being compared with other children around us and it is inferred that we 'should' be more like them, and if we are consistently not praised for who we are and for the things that we do get right, and we are regularly criticized when we don't meet the expectations of others, then invariably we become critical of ourselves and others. We can end up never having any sense of when we are enough and therefore we are left with a repeated sense of not feeling good enough.

As children we express ourselves freely. If a child says she wants to be a dancer, or an actress, and the parent says no, that's not a proper job, or you can't act, then that child's sense of self-expression could be damped down.

Children really know how to have fun. I notice with my grandkids; our bed becomes a trampoline, and the quilt becomes a tent to hide under. Before my personal growth and awareness of their self-expression I would have stopped them messing up my bed.

And often the adults around them will stop the child expressing themselves freely. Let's take dancing in the street with complete joy and happiness, being completely in the moment and unaware or uninhibited by those around them, and then suddenly an adult says 'Don't do that. What will people think or say?'

If this is said a few times then the child is likely to become self-conscious and fearful of judgment. This might show up later as an adult who wants to get up and dance at a social function but resists due to being worried about what people will say, and this can quite literally take the fun out of life.

We live in a competitive world. Some parents feel under pressure to encourage their children to do well in life for fear they will get left behind or excluded. And some have a fear of being judged as bad parents.

Comparing ourselves with each other is part of how we learn about ourselves. Others give us a reflection of what is or what could be, and that is normal and natural so long as we can find ways to truly see, hear and experience the whole of ourselves as us and not simply a reflection of how others perceive us.

It can start when we are children with parents talking about their children; they might start comparing their kids with each other within the family unit or outside. Noticing if one child is walking sooner than the other or starts talking sooner or later. It is normal. It is how the brain works. It is also natural for a parent to worry if their child is not developing in a way that is perhaps perceived as the norm. This is when intervention and specific support can be asked for.

The key is to do all this and be accepting of what is, as perfect and beautiful and okay all at the same time.

Due to the rules of society and expectations, most of our school systems do not allow us to express our uniqueness and our special gifts. Exams are about academic success or failure; they do not highlight what we are capable of from an early age. Some of my workshop attendees have described how some teachers have had a negative effect on them and now as adults it is still affecting them and they believe has resulted in their low sense of self-esteem.

If we hear negative comments, if we are labelled as not being good enough, naughty, disruptive, not clever, lazy etc, because we don't learn, think and behave as others believe is the norm, then we can grow up believing that's who we are and how we naturally wanted to respond is wrong. We can lose sight of our true self: our gifts and our true potential.

As children we can start to believe what adults tell us about ourselves. If we are given praise and acknowledgement when we do well and we are loved and accepted even when we don't do so well, then we grow up confident and happy to make mistakes as we learn and grow, which in turn means we can grow and develop into happy, confident adults.

It is important to mention that it is not always in our childhood that we lose a sense of who we are. Some children are raised completely protected and with the belief they are perfect as they are and they are rarely corrected or criticized. These children can often find adulthood very difficult because they suddenly find that not everyone else sees them as perfect like their parents and so they are suddenly faced with criticism and disapproval and it can come as a shock. Every gift, strength and uniqueness will be how we make a difference and add value and at the very same time those same gifts can be annoying to others.

If you are someone who is comparing yourself to others and you are inspired to be better, that is different to wishing you could be like them. If you are feeling that you are not as good, as clever, as presentable or as confident as other people, then it infers you are not aware of your current unique gifts that make you special and of value that you were born with. And yes, everyone does have them. You will not be exempt.

Going back to the analogy of the jigsaw puzzle, as you are one of the special, unique, important pieces, it is incomplete if you do not take your place and recognize your gifts. And if you don't recognize your gifts then how will you share them with the world and those that you are here to serve and inspire?

You are important and your contribution has an impact on the lives of others.

The poet Rumi says, 'Don't you know yet? It is your light that lights the world.'

It is our differences which make life interesting, exciting and challenging. Without the differences and challenges there would be no growth. Growth is one of the basic needs in nature and therefore in us as human beings since we are part of that nature.

Before my journey of personal growth and confidence, I used to compare myself to others and felt that I was not as good as others and I would wish I could look like them, or do what they could do. I remember at social functions staying by my husband's side most of the time, because I felt I would not be able to converse with them, and by standing with my husband I didn't have to speak if I didn't want to.

Over the years I have learnt to appreciate myself. Whenever I feel inferior, or I put someone on a pedestal, I remind myself that I am as good as the other person; I have my own gifts and they have their gifts. I have even learnt to express what I am good at, what I do well. In the past I would have thought that I was boasting.

I am also not afraid to be vulnerable. I can easily say if I am not good at something, or if I don't know something.

This confidence came from me slowly peeling away the onion layers, and getting rid of the beliefs that I did not want to believe anymore, the beliefs that did not serve me or make me feel happy. Without this development and conscious decision to change, I would not have been able to do what I do now. I wouldn't be able to do talks, run workshops and write this book. I had to peel off the layers of my conditioning by using all the tools I am sharing with you.

It is so important that you peel off these layers, so that you can really live life rather than just exist. You can have a life that feels fulfilling. And you can share your gifts and be of service to others who are going to benefit from you and your gifts. Then you will be shining your light, as Rumi says.

I love to dance, and one day I went to dinner in a restaurant with a group of people. The music was great, but no one was getting up to dance, so I just pulled the arm of one of my friends, and said let's dance. After that a couple of other ladies joined in. Later that evening one of them said to me that she got up because I did; she loves dancing but would not have had the courage to do so alone.

Even our so-called faults or negative traits are there for a reason, to serve others. There is a lovely story about a man who had to carry water from a water well to the town. He had two buckets, one on each end of a pole, which he carried on his shoulders. He did not realize that the bucket on his left had a tiny leak in it. The hole was getting bigger day by day.

One day, by the time he delivered the water, the leaking bucket was half full. He felt really bad about the loss of precious water and he felt he should have realized the bucket was faulty. Then when he looked back down the lane he saw something beautiful, and the people of the village also told him that he should not worry or feel bad, because as a result of his actions that side of the road was now in full bloom. You see, where the bucket was leaking it had been watering seeds and that resulted in lovely flowers growing. Everywhere else was so dry and nothing grew, but now the villagers were able to really enjoy walking along the road.

The moral of the story is that even our faults are there to serve until the point when maybe they are not needed and then we can change.

By not acknowledging your unique gifts, you are not likely to be expressing your full potential, and those around you will be missing out in receiving your contribution to them. Your true purpose in life may not be realized. This can lead to feeling stuck in a rut, unhappy, not worthy, depressed and unfulfilled.

How to express your unique, special gifts

> Imagine the core of an onion being your true self, your unique, special self, on this earth to express yourself and serve others with your gifts. The layers of the onion are the conditioning, the labels, beliefs, and experiences, the moulding we have as children. Now as adults using the

tools in this book, you can begin to peel off the layers that do not serve you to live your best life, and recognize and appreciate your own gifts and potential.

> Stop comparing yourself to others. Remind yourself that you are as good as anyone else; you have your own special talents and they have theirs. So you are equal to others and different.

> Stop judging yourself; instead accept yourself exactly as you are. Accept your positive qualities, as well as your negative qualities. None of us are good at everything. It is our differences that make us special. You can choose to change any habits of yours if you feel it will enhance you as a person. Anything you don't want to change, you just accept as your gift. Recently I became conscious that I was criticizing and comparing myself to my husband and one of my friends who also has grandchildren, both of whom take care of their needs, as well as the grandkids' needs, whereas I do everything for the grandchildren and when I get a free moment then I will think of myself. I tried to change myself to be like them, but except for a few important needs like taking my vitamins and drinking water, I found it difficult to be like them. Writing this chapter made me realize that my nature is that of being a supporter and this is what makes me unique and special and is my gift to my grandkids, and what my husband does is *his* gift.

> Accept praise and recognition from other people. Often we may make excuses or go into an explanation as to why it was not us but some other force that made it happen.

> Overcome your fears of judgment and rejection. Know that most of our fears are False Expectations Appearing Real. You may think someone is going to criticize you, or laugh at you; most people will not and if someone does, then for reasons of their own they have a need to do that and it really is nothing to do with you; you just triggered something in them, which is most likely from their childhood conditioning

and experiences, which creates their perception of things that happen around them.

> Change of conditioning and habits is a process, but as I've said before, if you keep the practice regular, you will see yourself transforming.

The benefits of expressing your uniqueness

When you learn to express your uniqueness you can expect to:

> Be kinder, more gentle and more loving with yourself.
> Be more forgiving of yourself and others.
> Have more compassion, as you will understand that others are also unique and special and we all have our conditioning from childhood that makes us react the way we do.
> Be comfortable in your own skin which allows you to be more vulnerable.
> Be able to accept criticism as simply another person's perception of you and not necessarily the truth.
> Develop a sense of pride in yourself and be more confident in things that you do well.
> Have the confidence to say and do what you want.
> Not be afraid of judgment.
> Be more creative.
> Be able to follow your life's purpose.
> Give other people the motivation and the courage to express themselves.
> Be much happier and have a sense of fulfilment.

'You are obligated to understand that you are unique in the world. There has never been anyone like you because, if there were, there would be no need for you to exist. You are an utterly new thing in creation. Your life goal is to realize this uniqueness.'

– Aaron Perlow

Reflection

Consider what makes you unique, what your special gifts are, the things you do well and others always come to you for. Perhaps refer back to Chapter 2 and the list of compliments others give you.

_____

_____

_____

Once you have a list of all your positive qualities, take time to celebrate and acknowledge them.

Make a list of what you are not good at.

_____

_____

_____

What gifts might you be bringing with what you believe you are not good at being or doing? Celebrate and acknowledge them.

Complete this sentence: I am unique because

_____

_____

CHAPTER SIX

Freedom to be fearful

'Many of our fears are tissue-paper-
thin, and a single courageous step
would carry us clear through them.'

- Brendan Francis

The emotion of fear is hardwired in all creatures. It is our defence mechanism to alert us to physical dangers, and to take action, so as to protect ourselves from real, physical danger. When we are in danger of being attacked, or need to save ourselves from a car rushing towards us, we need to respond in order to be safe and secure.

This is known as the flight, fight or freeze response. The body releases chemicals like adrenalin for us to have the energy to either fight or flee. This is of course when fear is a good thing. Once the response of fighting or fleeing is over the chemicals that had been released are no longer in the body.

This defence mechanism is not useful to us when it affects our self-worth, when it stops us living the life we would love to live. When it stops us having the freedom to be us.

These are fears of feeling rejected, or not being good enough, or fear of failure, fear of being judged, making decisions, fear of the unknown etc. The brain cannot differentiate between these emotional fears and the physically dangerous situations. The same fight and flight response takes place in the brain. And the body releases the chemicals the same as when we are faced with real danger.

With these emotional fears, we often do not seem to take any action. For example when you are at work, you feel that some people put you down by the way they speak to you, and you are afraid of saying or doing anything about it, but the fear will trigger the fight or flight response, and because you don't take action, the chemicals stay in the body without being used up. These chemicals then create symptoms like feeling unhappy, stuck, helpless, and could lead to you suffering from anxiety, depression and other illness.

Often the emotional fears are based on the perceptions and assumptions we make about what other people's actions, words, and tone of voice may mean. Many times these fears are False Evidence Appearing Real. We don't always know what other people's actions mean, but we have a story in our head according to our upbringing and past experiences.

These are the fears we can overcome when we have a better understanding about our fears. And there are many tools we can use so we don't live with these fears and stop living our lives to our full potential, if we really want the freedom to do, be and have what we want in life.

And if you don't deal with the fears and learn to be fearless you become paralysed and unable to do the things that you are destined to do or be. Not only do you lose out but also those that you are here to serve, support and inspire don't get to benefit from the whole of you being present and sharing your gifts and talents.

Benefits of dealing with fear

> You will feel much happier.
> You will be more relaxed.
> You will be able to achieve your potential and live your purpose.
> You will be able to live life to the full.
> You will have more fun.
> You will have more energy for others.
> You will have better health.
> You will be able to speak your truth.
> You will be able to appreciate and be grateful for more in your life.

How to have the freedom to be fearful

The best process I have found to deal with fear is in the book *Feel the Fear and Do It Anyway* by Dr Susan Jeffers, who sadly passed away in October 2012. Thanks to her book her wisdom lives on. Susan explains what she calls 'some truths about fears'. I have listed them below[7] in italics and share with you my own interpretation of each of them. I would like to thank Susan's husband, Mark Shelmerdine, for giving me permission to include them here for you.

1. The fear will never go away as long as I continue to grow.

Growth is one of our basic human needs. From the day we are born to the day we die, we are growing. As children we are growing our

FREEDOM to Be Me by Azmina Jiwa

mind, body and soul. As adults we mostly stop growing physically in terms of bones and the division of cells but the need to expand ourselves mentally and emotionally is ongoing. Every time we do something new we are likely to feel fear. So it's not so much about getting rid of fear in order to be able to follow our dreams; it's more about how are we going to do it in spite of feeling fearful.

> *2. The only way to get rid of the fear of doing something is to go out and do it.*

In order to grow, to do what we want to do in our life, to have the things we want to have, we have to be willing to go out of our comfort zone. If we continue to do what we have always done and don't take any risks then nothing changes. Going into the unknown can be very frightening, but we need to feel the fear and do it anyway. Once we have taken that first step, we begin to feel less fear, it starts to get easier, and eventually we get comfortable with whatever it is we are doing. It could be public speaking, dressing a certain way, being more assertive, taking a new class etc.

I want to share my experience of personal growth and overcoming my fear of public speaking, something I was absolutely terrified to do. To get out of my comfort zone I put myself forward to do a talk at the Mind Body Soul Exhibition. About an hour before I was due to give the talk, my heart was pounding and my hands were sweating. I wanted to cancel my talk but of course I did not; instead I sat somewhere and calmed myself by doing some meditation and visualization. It was an hour's talk, and there were about sixty people in the room. For the first fifteen minutes I was shaking and my knees were wobbly. As I saw people nodding and being attentive, I felt a bit more confident. When I finished it felt like I had done quite well. I celebrated by jumping about afterwards. For sure there were things I could have done better, but I did not let that take away my happiness for working through the fear. Since then I have spoken to many groups.

90 | CHAPTER SIX: Freedom to be fearful

*3. The only way to feel better about
myself is to go out and do it.*

Often we believe that we have to become confident, have all the knowledge, be slimmer, be perfect, before we can do what we want to do. But the truth is that often we have to do the things we want to, in order to build our confidence. For example, I had a friend who wanted to become an image consultant. She had done her course, but instead of starting to tell people that she was now an image consultant she felt the need to be perfect. She felt she had to build her confidence, and had to get all her samples, all the materials she needed, before she could get her business off the ground, whereas if she had started to get people interested and had booked a client, she would have had to get organized and get the material she needed and after a few clients she would have started to get more confident, and would have been able to feel good about herself.

Continuing with my story from (2) above, my confidence grew through offering to do talks to different groups and by saying yes when I was asked by other organizations.

*4. Not only am I going to experience fear whenever I
am on unfamiliar territory, but so is everyone else.*

Understanding that we are not alone and that others also experience fear when doing something unfamiliar can in itself bring comfort and ease the fear and pressure we put on ourselves because we think we shouldn't be so fearful in the first place. Great inventor Thomas Edison, who invented the light bulb, said, 'I have not failed. I've just found 10,000 ways that won't work.' Many of life's failures are people who did not realize how close they were to success when they gave up.

Abraham Lincoln tried ten times before he became president of the USA. Most successful people have felt fear, and still done what they wanted to do, and most have had more failures than those who are too fearful to even try.

> 5. Pushing through fear is less frightening than living with the underlying fear that comes from a feeling of helplessness.

Sometimes we just want to avoid feeling fear; it's not a comfortable feeling. In fact this feeling can be really intense when actually taking the risk to take that first step, but this is better than living with feeling stuck, unhappy or anxious. I lived for many years feeling unhappy, but as I started to take baby steps and saw that feeling happier is so much better, I realized that it really was not as terrible as I thought it would be.

There can be many underlying fears that prevent us from showing up as the person we are today. Let's look at some of the fears that affect so many of us and could be stopping you being yourself.

1. Fear of judgment

This fear can often stem from a belief or thought that we are not good enough or not the same as others. This can show up in many areas of our lives.

In relationships we might be afraid to say no because we feel we will be judged as selfish, or unhelpful. We can be afraid to be assertive or speak about our feelings in case we are rejected or judged as weak or emotional.

Perhaps you have a fear of public speaking because you are afraid you will say the wrong thing and people might laugh at you. At work maybe you are afraid to put your ideas forward in a meeting for fear your comments will be judged as being stupid.

In public you might be fearful at social functions and concerned that you are not doing things right. For example you might want to have a second helping of food, but you wait for others to do it first, or perhaps you worry about your outfit not being like others and therefore you think you will be judged for not fitting in.

We can all be guilty of judging ourselves and each other; it is part of being human. The key is to catch yourself and challenge your current thinking in order to overcome your fear of being judged. For me I was so consumed with self-judgment that I didn't have space to judge others and I assumed everyone was judging me.

Our beliefs influence how we make sense of what is happening and if something is different to how we expect it to be then we can judge it as being wrong. For example if I am in a group and lots of people are talking I might have a belief that people who talk are popular and judge myself as not being popular because I am much quieter.

We gain an understanding of how something is and we assume that to be the right way and then when we experience something that doesn't seem to fit that model we can judge it as being wrong rather than simply different.

What if everyone was feeling fearful of being judged just like us? They may also be worried that you are judging them. Or they are so busy thinking of their own issues, and what they are going to be doing next, that they have not even noticed you. In my experience when you focus on what you want and what works for you, you become more able to show up and be yourself without the fear of being judged by others.

How to deal with fear of judgment

> Become aware of your thoughts and feelings.
> Create a different positive thought/affirmation (see 'Positive affirmations' section in Chapter 1). Make these affirmations believable and specific to your thoughts and circumstances.
> Write the new thought on a card or Post-it note and have it where you can be reminded of it daily.

For example if it is in a meeting that you want to express an idea and your thoughts are about what a particular person in the meeting is going to say about it, then you can change your thoughts to 'Does it really matter if they think differently to me?' or 'My contribution may help others who are more open and non-judgmental' and in this way you will build your courage to express yourself more and more till it becomes a new habit.

2. Fear of failure

Society and school systems often don't encourage us to realize that there is no such thing as mistakes or failures, just outcomes and results. We seem to be growing up with the idea of having to be perfect first time, otherwise we have wasted time, money or resources which results in never even trying for fear of getting it wrong. And if we get as far as trying and we don't get it right first time, then we often judge ourselves as failures.

In reality there is no such thing as perfection. We can only attempt to do something with what we know in that moment in time in our life and in doing something we may or may not learn a new way.

Then in the next moment with the new knowledge we can do something or be something different. If the result is not exactly how we want it to be then we try again. Even in failing we have learned what doesn't work and that now adds to our knowledge and growth. Therefore it is better to try and fail than to never try because without trying we fail to learn and grow.

Procrastination can be one of the by-products of a fear of failing. We can come up with many excuses like 'I don't have time', 'It's too difficult', 'Is it really worth it?' or 'I am not ready at the moment'. When you challenge these thoughts they might be true and they might reveal a fear of failing.

How to deal with fear of failure

> Become aware of any beliefs you may have about yourself like you never get things right or you always fail.

> Identify your thoughts around these beliefs and change them to more positive thoughts. For example, you are saying to yourself, 'What if I am not up to standard in this new job I am being offered?' You could change it to 'I will never know unless I try; I can always learn new skills'. More on positive affirmations is explained in Chapter 1, Freedom to think differently.

> If it does not turn out how you wanted it to then consider what you have learned from the experience. Instead of thinking of it as a failure or a mistake, think about how it will inform future decisions. When you focus on the learning it is likely that you may come up with a new way of approaching the same problem to get a different outcome or result.

3. Fear of making wrong decisions

Because of our need to be perfect, not wanting to make mistakes, not wanting to be judged or fail, lose money or friends, or waste time, we have a battle in our mind about what to do when we are at a crossroads. These could be anything from little decisions about what to eat or what to buy, to some big decisions like a change to a career which you feel more passionate about than what you are doing now. Maybe your husband would love to move abroad.

When we are at the point of making a choice, we become fearful as the mind is going crazy with all the 'what ifs'. For example, if it is about moving abroad, the fear would be these what ifs: 'I don't make friends, I will be miserable, maybe there are no jobs there, what will my mother have to say about it, if I stay here we will never realize my dream, but I am well settled here'.

Often we will ask other people what they think we should do, and this could lead to even more confusion and tension. Sometimes we just give up the idea and give up on our dreams. Other times we may take a leap and make the decision to go for it, but then we may still keep wondering and worrying if it really is the right thing to do.

I learnt another way of looking at making decisions from Dr Susan Jeffers' book *Feel the Fear and Do It Anyway* where she teaches a 'No-Loss Model'[8]. She says 'each path has nothing but goodies along the way'. This thought brings relief and excitement.

So going with the same example of moving abroad, the 'goodies' could be to experience something new, have an opportunity to meet different people, have an adventure. And if it does not work out, there is a lot of learning that will have taken place, and you can return to your home country again.

I know someone who really wanted to go to Australia, but had a lot of fears around going. After attending my workshop she had the courage to take the risk and went. She thought she had nothing to lose. When I met her two years later, she told me that she would not have missed the experience for anything, but after two years felt she wanted to be back in her familiar environment.

How to deal with fear of making wrong decisions

> Make a list of advantages and disadvantages of each decision.
> Find out as much information as you can about the choices you have in front of you.
> Check in with your intuition (see Chapter 9).
> Trust your intuition.
> Once you have decided, let go of the fear by affirming the new experiences, learning and growth you will have.

'I have learnt that courage was not the absence of fear, but the triumph over it. The brave man is not he who does not feel afraid, but he who conquers that fear.'

– Nelson Mandela

Reflection

Make a list of what you would love to have, be or do and are not taking action to achieve.

_____

_____

_____

_____

Pick one that you feel you would like to work on first.

_____

Make a list of all the fears that come up for you which stop you taking action.

_____

_____

_____

Which ones might be false expectations appearing real to you?

_____

_____

_____

Ask yourself, are they really true?

Cross out the ones that are not really true.

For those that you think are true, write down 4 benefits to you of overcoming these fears.

_____

_____

_____

_____

What can you do to deal with your fears, using the tools above?

_____

_____

What are your present thoughts around the fear?

_____

_____

What could be a more positive thought?

_____

_____

CHAPTER SEVEN

Freedom to put yourself first

'Don't sacrifice yourself too much, because
if you sacrifice too much there's nothing else
you can give and nobody will care for you.'

– Karl Lagerfeld

To me putting ourselves first is essentially about loving, nurturing, praising and forgiving ourselves. Putting ourselves first is not about not taking other people's opinions into consideration. It's not about being self-centred or arrogant, and it is not about always getting your own way, or putting your needs first at the expense of others. It is about being considerate of your needs and the needs of others. It is about making your needs equal and as important as those you support. It is about clear communications and working in partnership to create an outcome that gets you both what you want. And sometimes that is a compromise that means win/win for both.

Putting yourself first and nurturing yourself is about making your needs of sleep, rest, health and your passions a priority. It's about doing things you would love to do without feeling guilty. It means loving yourself for who you are with your strengths and weakness. It also means praising yourself when you do something well, just as you praise others. It's about taking care of your needs before others, so you can serve them at your best. Think of it this way: if your health goes down the drain, are you even going to be around or available to help anyone else?

In my workshops I use a simple tool called the wheel of life. Basically I draw a circle and I divide it up into four main areas of our life. There are normally more areas, but for this exercise I just use four main ones.

> Work
> Family
> Me
> Social life

When I ask the participants which area of their life they consider as a priority, most of the time the answer given is work or family. It is very rare that anyone puts 'me' as a priority.

It seems most of us find it hard to put our needs before others, especially women. The messages we receive as we are growing up, when we do things to please ourselves first, are 'Don't be selfish', 'Family comes first', 'Put in extra hours at work to make a good impression', 'If you don't work hard you are not going to get anywhere in life', 'You are a good person when you give to others', and so on.

It is not often we will be told that self-care is as important as caring for others, or that we are special, that we can love ourselves, or forgive ourselves. We are not taught to be kind and gentle with ourselves – we are taught that we would be labelled as being self-centred.

In some cultures it is so ingrained in the way of life that women are there to serve their husbands and extended families. Traditionally women have had the role of caregiver within the family, and in doing that we may have put ourselves at the bottom of the list.

My mother was brought up in this kind of tradition. She was a people pleaser. She was ready to do everything others wanted her to do. She was always doing what my father wanted, not voicing her needs or what she would like to do. And I followed in her footsteps, until I realized that I was not happy doing this. I felt that I was existing and not really living life. When my daughter saw photos of me before my journey of self-discovery, she noticed that I looked very sad in them, whereas now in photos I look happy and lively.

When you don't put your needs before the needs of others around you, there is a tendency for others not to respect your needs, purely because they are not aware and assume that you are taking care of yourself. The message you are giving them by not expressing your needs is that it is okay for you to always be there for them and you don't need anything. It's easy for others to then take advantage of you.

There is no reason why there cannot be equal concern for others and us. When you treat yourself as a second-class citizen, you are sacrificing your own happiness, health and wellbeing, and physical and emotional needs.

When you have equal concern for yourself and others then you will be happy to help others because it will not be at the expense of your own health and happiness.

When you are constantly giving, when you are saying yes but really you want to say *no*, there is a tendency to be resentful towards the person you are helping. You may feel they are taking advantage of you and not caring about your needs. You will be serving half-heartedly. You will have less energy. In some cases you may not actually be there 100% for the other person, and so you are actually doing them a disservice. This could be friends, family members, or even at work.

So really I feel that being 'selfish' is good for you and others, just as you have to put your own oxygen mask on first before helping others in an emergency on an aeroplane.

And what can often happen, if you don't take care of your own needs, is that you can become unwell and unable to serve others, run down, depressed or simply exhausted, at which point others have to survive without you but you are not benefiting from the break because you are usually in bed.

The benefits of putting yourself first

- > More creative and productive
- > Better immune system
- > Able to give more to others
- > More love for others
- > Able to achieve more of your personal goals
- > More time to follow your passions
- > Able to communicate your needs

More creative and productive
You will be much more creative and productive if you take breaks, eat healthy lunches, have some snacks and if you are working, then leave work on time. People often prioritise work over having a break because they think they will not finish their work, but the truth is that after taking a break you will have more energy and be less stressed and finish faster than without having a break.

Better immune system

You immunity will be stronger, so you will have better health, and more energy. You may have noticed that when you have not given yourself enough rest you get sick. I certainly have noticed feeling weak and getting sore throats at these times.

Relationships with your children, partner, husband, family and friends will be better when you are not afraid to express your needs and your feelings. You will also give them the freedom to take care of themselves.

Able to give more to others

When you take care of yourself you have more energy to give. You are also more fun to be with. When I came back from my training with Dawn Breslin, because I had gone off and done what I wanted to do instead of always doing what my husband wanted, I came back feeling so alive and lively that my two children and husband noticed and said that it was so much nicer to be with me when I was like this.

More love for others

You will serve others with more love. As I mentioned earlier, if you do not meet your needs first then you are really not serving at your best, so that would be a good reason to approve of yourself when you have to say no. I understand that you may be very fearful of what others will think of you when you say no. But if you communicate how you are feeling now and when you have done what you need to do, you will be able to give them more. Most people would empathize with that. When you have taken care of yourself you will feel more centred, calmer and happier. You will probably smile more and that makes others smile. You will feel more vibrant, lively and fulfilled.

Able to achieve more of your personal goals

With your personal goals, you will be more creative, as you will have more time to yourself. When you are feeling happier, calm and relaxed your mind will be able to come up with new ideas for whatever goals you have for yourself personally, like eating more nutritious food or doing a workout or if you have projects at work or are self-employed. I have certainly found this to be true when I have time to myself: I'll often get ideas for my talks and workshops.

More time to follow your passions

By putting yourself first you will have time to follow your passions. Whatever you are passionate about could become your work, and therefore you will serve the world, with your purpose being fulfilled.

Able to communicate your needs

Communication and assertiveness are key as you begin the process of putting yourself first. Communicate what you need and want. It's not about asking permission of the other person. If you ask permission then the other person can easily say no. You just have to say what you want, what you would like to have and how you would like to be treated.

For example, in your workplace, you could say 'I will be taking half an hour break at 1pm as I find I work much better and I am more productive when I do that'. I don't think many people would argue with this statement. If you find that in spite of having said that someone comes and gives you work to be done at your break time, then you need to be assertive and remind them of your needs.

In my personal relationship with my husband, I rarely used to put myself first. I had stopped going out in the evenings if he was home, because he had said he did not like it if I was not home.

When I started my journeys back to having the freedom to be me, I started by acknowledging his feelings, then I expressed what I wanted and went ahead with my plans. I acknowledged that he didn't like to be home alone and that despite that I really wanted to go out. It was not easy at first. I had fears of rejection and felt guilty, but the more I got into the new habit, by using the tools I am offering in this book, the easier it became.

Now I have the freedom to live my life, and most of the time how I love it to be. I say 'most of the time' because, being human, we are on a journey and sometimes we do have to put the needs of others first, but it is just a case of ensuring it does not become the norm. Life throws challenges at us sometimes which can take us off track when it comes to providing ourselves with the appropriate amount of self-care and that is normal, but staying there is not good for prolonged lengths of time. For example when our children are young or at a time when a friend or relative is ill or grieving you might for a period of time put your needs on hold, but this is not sustainable long term.

By honouring my needs, and not fulfilling my husband's need for me to stay home, he learnt how to be okay home alone, when I was not there. This was his growth.

How to put yourself first

1. Look in the mirror and say to yourself 'I love you'. This will remind you that you are important and worthy. Loving yourself means accepting yourself just as you are.
2. Forgive yourself for what you feel you have done wrong or you are not doing for others.
3. Do something just for you that will energize you and make you feel good.
4. Praise yourself often.

In my early days of my personal development journey I was very emotional and tearful doing this exercise of looking in the mirror and saying to myself 'I love you', but I practised till I felt 'Yes, I do love myself' and doing that did remind me that I was important and worthy. I still sometimes follow this practice to remind myself that I am special.

'Until you value yourself, you won't value your time. Until you value your time, you will not do anything with it.'

– M. Scott Peck

Reflection

Where and when are you allowing other people's needs to come before your own needs?

_____

_____

_____

What baby steps can you take to start the process of putting yourself first?

_____

_____

Look in the mirror and say to yourself 'I love you'.

Journal how you feel whenever you do this exercise. Practise it till you get comfortable with the exercise and feel love for yourself.

Write 5 things you can praise yourself for.

1. _____

2. _____

3. _____

4. _____

5. _____

How did it feel to give yourself praise?

_____

_____

_____

What can you say to yourself to forgive yourself whenever you feel guilty?

_____

_____

_____

CHAPTER EIGHT

Freedom to speak your truth

'Strength comes from living your
truth. To be true and authentic is your
path to happiness, peace, and joy.'

– Anonymous

Speaking your truth is about having no shame about who you are. It does at times mean you may feel vulnerable and it is about being comfortable with your humanness. It is about being comfortable with your strengths and your weaknesses in equal measure. It is about being okay with being imperfect. To speak your truth is to be authentic, honest, and sincere. It is not about changing the situation or the outcome; it is just about speaking honestly about how you feel. It is not about being right; it's about your version and how you see it, hear it and feel it.

When we are babies and very young children we are born to speak the truth. From the time we are born we want love and a sense of belonging.

As very young children we are able to do, be and say how we feel and what we want. We don't worry about being perfect or what others think. We don't care if our clothes are dirty and we will dance and skip in the street or at the supermarket. Children, and therefore all of us, are born with the freedom to speak our truth and so were you.

From the age of three or four years old, children can start to feel they are not good enough as they become aware there is a right and a wrong way to do or be.

Simple acts like a parent wanting to protect their child could result in the child experiencing shame for speaking their truth and being their authentic self. By taking over and doing things for our children they can infer they are not capable and therefore lose confidence in their ability and the courage to speak their truth.

If you experience ridicule or being told off when you are being honest and truthful, as a child or adult you are likely to shut down your true feelings and true expressions. This can for some result in you building an imaginary wall around you as protection from future pain and hurt and can prevent you from speaking openly and honestly again.

As an adult, many of us might have grown up thinking that speaking up is rude and speaking out is disrespectful; you might have been taught that being emotional is a sign of weakness. This can then inhibit us from being and doing what we want. We might feel embarrassed and afraid of being our natural self and actually saying what we are thinking or feeling.

As humans we have a strong sense of wanting to be accepted, so many would rather pretend to be something they are not than show their true self and be rejected by others. This can result in you putting pressure on yourself to be perfect in the eyes of others. Our tendency can be to make excuses, or to call ourselves 'dumb' or 'stupid'. We start to label ourselves.

In the workplace, this might result in you covering up your mistakes and overworking to gain approval and a sense of self-worth. You may even start blaming others for not allowing you to speak up and share what you think is best.

In your social life, if you are invited to a party, and you don't feel like going, you might make up an excuse or end up going and not enjoying it. Not feeling free to speak your truth could prevent you from going to new places or classes in case you get it wrong.

Dr Brené Brown's *The Power of Vulnerability*[9] debunks some myths about vulnerability, the most popular being that vulnerability is a sign of weakness. When we think of times that we have felt vulnerable or emotionally exposed, we are actually recalling times of great courage, even though sometimes at the time it may not have felt so courageous.

As I write this book I am being reminded of how many times I have been fearful and yet I have gone on to achieve so much because I spoke my truth despite that fear. As I wrote the chapter about my story I remembered just how often I have had that real pull inside that wouldn't go away and I knew I had to do something and so I spoke my truth. Since learning to speak my truth I have discovered that I now hear my intuition more and more and that calling is getting stronger and stronger which means I feel more aligned and on purpose more of the time.

Dr Brené Brown also says 'Vulnerability is the birthplace of love, belonging, joy, courage, empathy, and creativity'[10]. Once you have allowed yourself to speak your truth a few times, you are more likely to feel free to express yourself, more often and much more easily.

This does require you to have courage and determination to change your current patterns of behaviour. It is about taking responsibility for your own experience whatever the outcome.

What I have noticed is that when I fail to show up as the whole of me and I am not entirely honest, I invite others to do the same. This means that when each of us fail to speak our truth we not only hold ourselves back but we encourage others to do the same. This can prevent us from feeling truly and authentically connected with those we love and care for.

The benefits of speaking your truth

> Speaking your truth can liberate you.
> It can change the lives of those around you.
> It can bring you closer to people, and it can also distance you from those who are not open to you being honest with them and therefore prevent you from growing and being you. And it will distance you from those who blame others for their experience in life.
> It can teach you to know and accept yourself just as you are at any point and time in your life which means you will be kinder and more compassionate and accepting of yourself. The simple act of deciding to speak your truth means you do have to clarify what that is for you and in doing so you gain clarity of your own thoughts and learn to communicate them to others with love. I talked more about this in Chapter 2, Freedom to accept yourself. And when you accept yourself you are less concerned about whether others accept you or not and therefore you have less fear.
> Speaking your truth encourages you to be honest about your strengths and mindful of when those same strengths can be frustrating to others. For example the fact I am a good listener and willing to be quiet and listen is one of my strengths and it can be frustrating for myself and others when I don't speak up

and share my own opinions, thoughts and feelings because it makes it difficult for others to understand me.

> You will become consciously aware of your feelings and fears, like rejection, or not being good enough or being judged by others in a negative way, which means you have choice and can do something about them. If you realize you have a belief that does not serve you and those you love then you can change it as we discussed in Chapter 1, Freedom to think differently.

> You will feel more peace and happiness.

> You will be able to say 'no' when before you would have said 'yes'.

> You might feel able to step out of your comfort zone and go to new places or classes and experience new things.

> You will be able to do things you have always wanted to do but didn't because you feared being judged and therefore never asked.

> You will listen to your intuition. If you feel something is right at the core of you then that is the right thing to do and as you practise speaking your truth you will hear this more and more.

> When you overcome the fear of being vulnerable, of speaking your truth, you will become more authentic which means you will be more at peace with yourself.

> You will also be able to speak up and admit your mistakes, accept your imperfections, and ask for forgiveness, which frees you of past regrets and guilt.

> You will empathize much more with others because you will be more aware of how difficult it can be to speak your truth and to be honest about how you feel. So you can and will make it easier for others to speak their truth and share truthfully how they feel.

> Others are more likely to trust you more because they feel they always know where they stand with you because they can trust you to tell them what you want and need.

> You can expect to be more decisive and that can make other people more comfortable with your decisions and being around you.
> You should have greater and deeper connections with people, as being vulnerable makes you more human and approachable, and gives other people permission to be vulnerable too.
> You are likely to be less concerned about the opinion of others and therefore you are likely to be less defensive because you know your truth and are not worried about the judgment of others.
> You will be able to have new experiences and make new friends, as people find you genuine.
> It reduces long-term stress. Instead of worrying about how and what you will say so you don't look bad or you don't hurt the other person, all you have to do is be honest, in a loving way. I think by being vulnerable we are showing we are human. We don't only liberate ourselves, but we also allow others to be honest and we accept others without judgment more.

How to speak your truth

Firstly become aware when you are not speaking your truth. This may be in the form of a white lie, an excuse you are making, saying yes when you want to say no. It could be as simple as saying you can't afford something when the truth is you don't like it or want it.

Identify the fear that led you not to be completely honest. It may be fear of being judged, or told off, or not wanting to upset someone or hurt their feelings.

Create an affirmation which will help to build your courage to speak your truth, for example 'Speaking my truth frees me, and gives me more energy'.

Visualizing yourself expressing your truth can also be very powerful. You do this imagining yourself speaking with the person that you would normally be afraid of being completely honest with. This time you are being honest in your imagination. See yourself; hear what you are saying and feel how it feels to speak the truth. When we visualize, we are practising the new habit we want, as our mind cannot tell the difference between visualizing and reality.

Take baby steps by practising with people you feel comfortable with. It helps to say how you feel by communicating with 'I', for example, 'I feel I need to listen to my body' and 'I can see you would really like me to come and I feel _____'.

Remind yourself the discomfort you feel is not going to last long and will go once speaking your truth becomes a new habit.

One of the greatest challenges when it comes to speaking our truth is communicating it in a way that is less likely to result in an adverse response. It takes courage to speak up and if every time you do someone else reacts badly you might recoil and give up. In fact it might be why you stopped speaking your truth in the first place.

Drama free feedback

Sheryl Andrews, author of *Manage Your Critic – From Overwhelm to Clarity in 7 Steps*[11], refers to the drama free feedback model which is made up of four great questions that help us to separate the story we tell ourselves so that we can articulate the facts. (You can find the questions in the Reflection at the end of this chapter.)

When we take time to separate the facts from the fiction we are communicating what is actually happening and how that is making us feel which is often based on our beliefs and past experiences.

For example you might see your child lying on the sofa. The fact is they are lying on the sofa. The story could be that you think they are being lazy and you might believe they are resting. The behaviour is the same but the story is different based on how you make sense of what you see and hear.

When you separate fact from your story/inference and you accept it is just that, your story then is easier to communicate.

Sometimes the clarity you gain from this activity might mean you don't need to say anything to anyone else because you have spoken the truth to yourself. If you do have to, speak the truth with someone else, and be patient and kind with yourself. It can take time to develop the ability to state our truth without judging or accusing others. Start with small things and ensure you are calm and coming from a place of love, not frustration, fear or anger.

Then get curious about the impact that has on you. Let's take the son on the sofa. When you see and hear him lying on the sofa and you think he is being lazy, what is the impact on you? Maybe you feel jealous and wish you could rest; maybe you worry that others will think you are a bad mother and maybe you worry that he will get depressed or something worse.

Notice what you notice and be willing to explore further.

Once you have clarity of:

> What you hear and see
> The story you make up that makes sense of it
> The impact on you

Then you can decide, what you would like to have happen?

When we communicate our truth from this perspective it is more likely to be heard although it cannot be guaranteed, as we never know what is happening for the other person as we share our version of events. But it is a great starting point to start to have more constructive conversations about what you want and what is not working for you and why.

In this example of the son lying on the sofa, you might have said you are being lazy or stop being so lazy. Whilst that is you speaking your truth, it is likely to cause drama. Either the son will accuse you of something you do or don't do, or he might ignore you as there is no request for something different or he might do 'something' in the moment to appease you but it is unlikely the behaviour will be a long-term change.

Using the drama free feedback model you might say: When I see you lying on the sofa I see that as being lazy and the impact on me is I feel resentful when I have so much to do. And what I would like is some help so that I can also have some time to lie on the sofa. In this example it is more likely to result in a conversation about the help wanted.

'Authenticity is a collection of choices that we have to make every day. It's about the choice to show up and be real. The choice to be honest. The choice to let our true selves be seen.'

–Brené Brown

Reflection

Make a list of:

> When you feel you are not being authentic.

_____

_____

_____

> Where and when you do not speak your truth.

_____

_____

_____

> When you feel embarrassed, and therefore make up a story (just be honest here with yourself; it is only you that is listening right now and that is where the freedom to be you starts).

_____

_____

_____

> When you are afraid of sharing how you truly feel.

_____

_____

_____

> Who you are most afraid to share your thoughts and feelings with.

_____

_____

_____

Then with each example ask yourself these drama free feedback questions:

> What would I like to have happen?
> How do I need to be?

Drama free feedback

Experiment with asking yourself the drama free feedback questions in order to set yourself up with greater clarity before speaking your truth. Especially if you want to avoid the drama caused by judging or accusing others.

> What I hear and see is

_____

_____

_____

> **What I infer from that is**

_____

_____

_____

> **The impact on me is**

_____

_____

_____

> **What I would like to have happen is**

_____

_____

_____

CHAPTER NINE

Freedom to listen to your intuition

'Don't let the noise of others' opinions drown out your inner voice. And most important, have the courage to follow your heart, and intuition. They somehow know what you truly want to become.'
– *Steve Jobs*

The word intuition comes from the Latin *intuir*, which appropriately means 'knowledge from within'. It has been called by many different names like gut feeling, higher voice, sixth sense, inner feeling, instinct, the voice of our soul, and sometimes it is referred to as spiritual guidance.

Science of the brain shows that the right side of our brain is responsible for our intuition, imagination and creativity, and the left side brain is for logic, rationality, fear and the analytical.

each of us is born with the ability to be intuitive. Yet it some people have a highly developed intuition whilst others hardly ever use it, or even know that it's there, and there are those that are somewhere in between.

Professor Gerard Hodgkinson[12] says intuitive judgments are 'based on rapid, non-conscious evaluation of internal and external information'. This shows that our instincts tell us what we need to know before our conscious mind catches it. So we can probably say that our intuition is our own internal personal GPS, with 24/7 access.

Through the understanding of neuro-linguistic studies we know that intuition can come in three different ways. Some of us will sense it through feelings, some will see it as visions or images and others will hear it as thoughts.

Generally in our society we are encouraged to use our reasoning, rational, logical brain, and therefore we can easily miss out on our intuitive guidance. Another reason we might miss out on our intuition is due to fear. Our fear is a left brain activity, so if we are living with fear of failure or judgment then we can fail to connect with our intuition because the fear takes over.

Say you have a decision to make, your intuition will be there if you listen carefully and yet thoughts like 'What if it is the wrong decision?' or 'What will others say?' and all that mind chatter can take over and then you either don't know what to do or you end up doing what you think others want you to do. This is when you are listening to the logical left side of your brain without truly listening to the right side of your brain.

There are many recorded incidences where intuition prevented catastrophes and cases of remarkable recoveries. At times of acute pressure or danger where conscious analysis is difficult, people have used intuition to survive.

Science tells us that only 20% of the brain's grey matter is used for conscious thoughts, whereas 80% is dedicated to non-conscious thoughts. Intuition bridges the gap between the conscious and non-conscious. Albert Einstein once said that intuition is our most valuable asset, and one of our most unused senses.

It is a well-known fact that Henry Ford made all his business decisions based on his intuition. It is said that our intuition's most important role is to alert us to the path, people, and circumstances that we will uniquely find fulfilling.

We often hesitate to follow our intuition because we are afraid of the changes we may need to make to follow our true path.

Because I was living with so much fear, my intuition was almost completely shut down. When someone would say to me that they had a gut feeling, or that they had a knowing about something, I just could not understand what they meant. When I learnt that we all have intuition and I realized that mine came through as a thought, I started to pay more attention to my first thought about decisions I had to make, and started to follow my intuition as much as I could. It is still work in progress for me.

When we don't learn or trust enough to listen to our intuition, we miss out on a great natural gift of receiving inner guidance to lead us to truth, to our best life that we could have.

How to develop your intuition

Recognize it

Intuition is like working a muscle: the more you exercise it, the stronger it gets and the first thing is to learn how to recognize your intuition. Here are some ways that work for me.

When you have to make decisions or have a question you want a solution to, notice what happens first. Do you have a feeling, or thought, or maybe a vision?

Maybe you have had an experience where you had an overwhelming sense that something is right and you know it but can't always describe it logically. That is intuition. Firstly, become aware of when you get this feeling, thought or vision.

Make a note of what is happening. Maybe you can locate your intuition? Is it inside you or outside you? Does it have a shape or size? Collect as much information as you can about your intuition. The more familiar you become with how your intuition works the easier it will become to use it.

As you become more aware of your intuition, you may notice other physiological changes; maybe your heart starts pounding, or your palms begin to sweat, maybe a knot in your gut, or your heart feels like it is growing. When you start to pay more attention to all those clues, then you will begin to recognize it and trust it as your true guidance system.

Also be aware of your self critic and fear which will creep in. You need to put that aside to follow your intuition.

Practise
You might start by practising in small ways, like which road to take or what to order at the restaurant. Pay attention to the first thing that comes to mind, your hunches, gut feelings and thoughts.

Meditation helps to quiet our mind, and enables us to listen to the inner guidance. Studies of the brain have shown that meditators have more grey matter related to sensitivity to the body's signals and sensory processing.

Writing or journalling can help us hear our own inner thoughts, if we allow ourselves to write without editing or self-correcting. Just write the first thing that comes to mind and allow the words to flow. This can help us to tap into feelings and thoughts and once you have written them down it is like the mind is freed and intuition can come into play with new insights.

Practise being present in this moment right now. Instead of your mind thinking about the past or future, bring it back to now and check in with your inner feelings, voice or vision.

You can even talk to your higher self to get answers by asking questions and then listening carefully for the response.

Now when it comes to intuition I should clarify that following our intuition does not mean that we will always have a pleasant experience, and we may start to question as to whether it was the right choice. Often this is meant to lead us to some learning. And sometimes learning is uncomfortable, especially if it is a lesson we have had presented to us time and time again and yet we don't seem to be learning the lesson. It can be frustrating to find ourselves feeling that we are going around in circles and back to where we started. I would argue that is because we are not truly listening and learning the lesson and so it repeats until we do.

There is a process called kinesiology that tests muscles to assess what your body thinks and feels about a particular thing. Whilst I am not an expert in this field, I have seen a demonstration of the arm method and I have found it useful at times to listen to my own intuition.

The arm method does require help from someone else. You have to raise your arm out to the side, at shoulder height, and your helper will place two fingers on your arm and push down gently to test the resistance in your arm. You might test this with something you know the answer to, such as is my hair blond? If your body agrees then the arm will be strong and if the body disagrees the arm will be weak and your helper will find it much easier to push the arm down.

I have seen this method used for all kinds of things like asking 'Should I go to the party?' or 'Should I eat peanuts?' When testing foods you can hold the food in one hand and hold out the opposite and simply test resistance.

Another one I personally like to use is to find your balance with your feet firmly on the ground, in a neutral position. Ask the question and if the body sways forward it is a yes and if it sways backwards then it is a no. You may not find this very easy in the beginning, and sometimes it is easier with a friend who can observe your movements but with practice, you can become more aware of your body's reaction.

Benefits of using our intuition

> Making decisions becomes easier.
> There is a greater feeling of being in flow with life and more relaxed, rather than feeling life is a struggle.
> You will experience increased creativity.
> Balancing of the left and right brain will give you a complete perspective on issues.
> You will have greater confidence to follow your life's purpose.

'Intuition is always right in at least two ways, it is always in response to something, it always has your best interest at heart.'

– Gavin de Becker

Reflection

Are you aware of your intuition?

_____

Have you noticed how your intuition comes to you? Is it vision, a thought or a feeling in your body?

_____

_____

_____

How much do you listen to your intuition?

_____

_____

_____

_____

List different areas of your life where you could use your intuition.

_____

_____

_____

_____

When you act on your intuition then what happens?

_____

_____

_____

_____

How do you feel when you use your intuition?

_____

_____

_____

_____

CHAPTER TEN

Freedom to live your life purpose

'Let the beauty of what you
love be what you do.'
- Rumi

ahlil Gibran said, 'When you are born your work is placed in your heart.' I believe that everyone has a life purpose, and it is often something we feel passionate about doing or a sense of calling. It is our birthright. The fact that we are born is itself a gift we have been given and a talent to express so that we can serve others with that gift.

As I said in Chapter 5, Freedom to be special and unique, you are one of the pieces in the big jigsaw puzzle, and each piece is connected to the others. Your unique gifts and talents are your contribution to those who are connected to you and all the other pieces in the jigsaw puzzle.

When you live a purposeful life, it gives meaning to everything you do and have. It is the thing that you want to jump out of bed for. It is something you will stick with even when the going gets tough, as life is full of ups and downs.

Some people have a clear vision of what they would love to do in their life; for some the vision is unclear. You may not know what your gifts are and you may not acknowledge those things that you are good at.

There are various reasons for that. Maybe as a child, you expressed your dream job but society, teachers or your parents ridiculed it, saying things like 'That is not a real job'. We can take on these beliefs which then prevent us from listening to our calling and our purpose. We would be inclined to push our dreams aside and follow what others say to us. Many grow up with the belief that work is something you do to have a status or make lots of money. Sometimes due to peer pressure we feel we have to be doing what our friends are doing.

The work you end up doing may be fine; you may be good at the job, but you may not be enjoying what you are doing. Something will be missing; you might be struggling with it, and it lacks a sense of fulfilment.

Whilst I was writing this chapter on holiday in the Philippines, I asked the deputy manager of the hotel why she chose this work, and she told me that it was because her mother did not want her to leave and what she would have loved to do was to study architecture but this was not available in her area, so she did a course in hospitality instead. Although she enjoyed her job, she said that she would be happier if she could do what she wanted.

According to research by the London School of Business and Finance[13], 47% of people want to change jobs, due to lack of job satisfaction. Interestingly, having job satisfaction was deemed more important than pay.

I have also found that many people who attend my workshops are not happy with the work they are doing. Some say they do not know what they want to do. And others are fearful of making the changes, in case it does not work out with a new job. A huge sense of insecurity sets in with lots of 'what ifs'. 'What if I cannot pay all the expenses like the mortgage?' is often the biggest worry that stops people from taking action.

When we don't do a job we love or the things we enjoy in our lives, then life can feel out of balance. There is no fun or excitement. It is like being on the treadmill, just going through the process of doing the tasks that need to be done for the sake of money to pay bills, or cooking for the family, or whatever you feel you must do in order to survive. Living like this without passion for what you are doing can leave you feeling exhausted.

And I do believe it is never too late to listen to your intuition and undo the beliefs and thoughts that hold you back from aligning yourself with your passion and purpose. It's never too late to live your life with purpose. In his book, *10 Secrets to Success and Inner Peace*, Wayne Dyer said 'Do not die with your music still in you'. He also quoted Kahlil Gibran, author of the book *The Prophet*, saying 'when you are born, your work is placed in your heart'[14].

I see our music as that niggle, feeling or voice coming from deep within our heart or soul, that is pushing us to do more of what we love. When we truly listen to the intuitive part of us we hear how we add value and make a difference, to know that we have a purpose and we have always been on purpose. If we do not make that part of us stronger then the left brain activity takes over with fear of change and over analysing everything that comes up.

And your purpose does not have to be something grand; it simply has to give you pleasure, fulfilment and help you be of service to others. I recently heard an example of a cleaner who really appreciated that she could help a family to have a clean home; this was her purpose. She loved that her role allowed the parents to spend more time with their families and it gave her immense joy.

So, your purpose may be loving keeping people's houses clean, taking care of children, picking up rubbish, being a doctor or a banker. If you're not working outside the home in order to make a living, you can still express your purpose and passions by doing things you love doing like gardening or cooking – whatever you enjoy and feel energized by.

If you don't find your purpose you live a life that others want for you. You lose out on feeling fulfilled and happy. People around you miss out on your unique gifts that are meant to serve them.

How to find your purpose

1. Create some time in stillness and ask the questions, What am I here for? What is my purpose? What do people trust me to do? What do I love? When am I happiest?

   The more you practise this the more the ideas, visions, feelings and thoughts will start flowing in, maybe not instantly.

2. Start noticing what makes you happy. What gives you a feeling of fulfilment? When you see something or someone, maybe on television for example, and your heart jumps at the idea and you hear yourself thinking how you would love to do that or be that, notice it and be curious.

3. Build your courage muscle by doing something every day that scares you and takes you beyond your comfort zone.

Also trust your ability and the universe to support you. Know that once you create an intention then the Law of Attraction is set into motion.

4. Make changes gradually. You don't have to lose all that you have now, but you can gradually transition from where you are to where you want to be. If you have an office job Monday to Friday and you want to be a massage therapist, start by talking to people about it. Perhaps work one weekend a month to start with, and then you may reduce your hours at work. I have come across so many people who seem to think they have to leave their job before they can start doing what they love, but that's not the case.

5. Create a vision board. You can do a vision board for any area of your life. Take poster paper, or any paper size of A4 and above. Then get some magazines which appeal to you. Focus on what you would love to do for work, what you would like to introduce into your life and what might energize you, and make an intention to find pictures and words that resonate with you in the magazine. Once you have a few, stick them on the paper and make a lovely collage. Then put this somewhere that you see it often. It is a great way of learning to trust your intuition too as you will be attracted to certain words and images through this process. Having it in sight will keep you focused on what you want; this can be motivating and it can also help you start to notice the things you already have that you love as more things come into your life.

My daughter attended my very first workshop in 2004 and now she is doing all the things she put on her vision board. She is a journalist; she started her career with newspapers and then documentaries with a TV channel and then moved on to working for a media company doing positive stories, including flying to several countries in Africa to do this.

6. Visualize your goal, which means taking time to imagine yourself doing more of what you love and living a life with purpose. Once you have identified what you would love to be doing, taking time to imagine yourself doing it gives your brain more information and resources to identify opportunities. Imagine yourself as though you have already achieved your goal. In your mind's eye, take yourself to this place, and see yourself in the picture as if you are there right now instead of where you are sitting or sleeping (it is more powerful this way than to see it as a movie on a screen). Don't worry if you do not have very strong visual tendencies; not everyone does, which is why tools like the vision board are great for cultivating images. See your surroundings exactly how you would like them to be. Make it colourful and large, then bring it closer to you. Now listen for all the sounds there would be in this environment. You may be saying something and listening to what others may be saying or you may hear other sounds around you. Now feel how it feels to be doing what you love doing. Really feel it in every cell of your body and then double the feelings in your body. Here is a link www.azminajiwa.com/resources to a guided visualization I have created for you.

7. Ask the right questions. Here are four questions you may find it useful to ask yourself:

> If I had only a year to live what would I do? This will give you a clue as to what is really important to you and what you would love to do.
> If time, money and resources were not an issue and I could do whatever I wanted, what would it be?
> What problem do I care about that I can do something about?
> What would I like to have people remember me for when I am gone?

8. Say yes to when life happens. Sometimes in our most challenging times of our life when unforeseen circumstances happen, that's when we find our purpose. I found teaching personal development through my feeling down and worthless and overcoming it. Victor Frankl, in *Man's Search for Meaning*, wrote about the meaning of life after surviving the holocaust. My cousin Azim Khamisa found his purpose after the tragic murder of his only son by a gang member who was only 14 years old as his initiation to the gang. My cousin saw both the murderer and his son as victims. This realization and being able to forgive led him to set up a foundation which goes into schools, teaching non-violence, love and compassion. He also teaches his '4 steps to forgiveness' process.

9. Think outside the box. There may be things you do which you love, but have the belief that you cannot earn money from doing. A very long time ago, before the internet and blogs, I read a story in a magazine about a woman who loved to watch soaps like *EastEnders* and *Emmerdale* and she started writing about the series for people who may have missed them, and that is how she made money out of doing what she loved.

Benefits of living with purpose

> A greater sense of fulfilment
> Being more productive
> Feeling happier and relaxed and enjoying life more
> Succeeding
> Inspiring others and making a difference to their lives
> Better health
> More motivation and energy

'The heart of human excellence often begins to beat when you discover a pursuit that absorbs you, frees you, challenges you, or gives you a sense of meaning, joy, or passion.'

– Terry Orlick

Reflection

Are you doing what you enjoy, love or are passionate about?

_____

If not then make a list of what is stopping you (beliefs, fears, not knowing what you want to do).

_____

_____

_____

_____

Challenge your thoughts – are they true?

Create an affirmation to support you to move towards your purpose.

_____

_____

_____

_____

Answer the questions from the section on 'How to find your purpose' in this chapter.

What other tools from this chapter could you put into practice, such as visualization, a vision board or meditation?

_____

_____

_____

_____

When you have a sense of what you would love to do, ask yourself 'What is the very first step I need to take to make my purpose a reality?'

_____

_____

_____

_____

CHAPTER ELEVEN

Freedom to live a balanced life

'We have overstretched our personal
boundaries and forgotten that
true happiness comes from living
an authentic life fueled with a
sense of purpose and balance.'

- Oprah Winfrey

A balanced life is a life where you are not just focusing on one or two areas of your life but paying attention to all aspects of your life. There are several aspects in our life to consider and these will be different for different people. And they will be different at different times of our lives depending on what our priorities are, for example if you have children your priorities will be different to when you retire.

And not only do you need to spend enough time in that area of your life, but you should be there 100% in mind and body. As Dr Susan Jeffers says, 'be there 100% and know that you are important'[15]. If you are at home but your mind is on the work you have to do, or maybe you are at work and you are feeling guilty that you should be with your children, then you are not there 100%, therefore not living a balanced life.

Generally though, the aspects are:

> **Myself** – We have ourselves and our own emotional needs, such as personal development.
> **Relationships** – We have family, which may consist of our children and spouse, our parents and extended family.
> **Social** – We have friends and other social interests.
> **Work** – We have our work, career, parenting...
> **Contribution** – By nature we feel good when we give to others, so we have the side of us that wants to contribute in some way, maybe volunteering or giving items, money etc.
> **Spiritual** – We have a soul, our higher self, which helps us to feel calm and centred. It's our inner guidance system – our intuition.
> **Health** – We have our physical body that needs to have exercise and healthy food. It's important to have good health to enjoy life and to enable you to do things that excite you like travelling, or playing with your kids.
> **Finances** – They give us the security for fulfilling our basic needs.

Focusing too much time on one area of your life can firstly have a domino effect and impact all other areas. For example if you are someone who has a family, say children, husband and maybe parents that you are caring for, and you spend most of your time taking care of everyone else, this then does not give you time to take care of yourself. This can lead to you being tired and emotionally drained and could impact your health.

Or if you spend too much time at work this might result in you not having time for friends, families or hobbies that re-energize you.

This can lead to you being stressed and tired and is likely to have a negative impact on your relationship with your partner or spouse.

Secondly, if for some reason you lose your job, or your children leave home, you could feel devastated and maybe even depressed. You would find it more difficult to deal with the loss, whereas when you have a more balanced life, you will have other aspects of your life that are also important to you. These will support you emotionally and that way you will be able to survive the change much better.

There is an exercise that can help you see how balanced your life is. In essence you draw a circle and you create as many sections as you feel are appropriate to represent the core areas in your life and then you mark along the axes 1-10. Then you give each aspect of your life a score, with 10 being perfect and it couldn't be any better, and 0 not happening at all.

If we assume a balanced life it means that all aspects have a similar score and then the wheel can move smoothly, whereas when one area of our life is getting more focus than the other the wheel looks irregular and generally represents a life that feels out of balance.

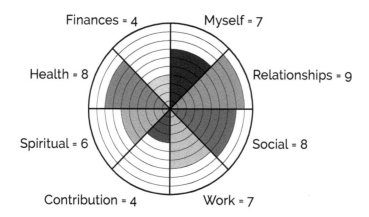

If the above were the wheel on our bicycle or our car, we would be having a very bumpy ride and we just would not put up with it. The car or bicycle would be at the garage to put it right very fast. But when it comes to our own life being bumpy, we do have a tendency to just plod along. When our life is not working we sometimes don't even know it is not working because of our beliefs and habits telling us that is how it should be, and at other times we are too afraid to make changes.

It is important to remember that only we can balance our life; others cannot do it for us. If you are feeling exhausted, mentally stressed, physically unfit or spending too many hours at work then you know that your life is out of balance and you have to be the one to change something.

If you don't get your life in balance then not only you will suffer but also those you are here to serve, whether that is your family or those that you are on the planet to support with your gifts and talents.

How to live a balanced life

1. To create a more balanced life, assess your life as it is now. Look at each area of your life and see how much time and attention you are giving each area.

2. How happy do you feel in that area of your life? You would grade yourself between 0 and 10, with 0 being not engaging in that area of life to 10 where you are happy with the time you spend in this area.

3. Of course it is not practical to be 10 in all the areas as we have different priorities in life, but once you have identified which areas you feel are out of balance you can create an intention or a goal on how you would like that area of your life to be.

4. Ask yourself 'What is the first step I need to take?', and the next step and so on. Be specific, so for example if it is to exercise, then what type of exercise, where will you exercise and when will you exercise.

5. Be kind and gentle with yourself; change invariably does not happen overnight. Forgive yourself for not being perfect. Take care of your needs first; that way you have more energy to do things for others. Do take enough rest. Do what you enjoy. Spend some quiet time to centre yourself. Be kind and forgiving to yourself.

Benefits of living a balanced life

> Health and wellbeing will be improved.
> You will be more productive.
> You will feel less stressed.
> Your relationships will be better.
> You will have greater emotional connection with yourself and others.
> You will be much happier and more peaceful.

Some points to consider when you fill out your wheel of balance below in the 'Reflection' section

Yourself – Become aware of your own needs – what would you love to do that would energize you. Spend time doing at least one thing for yourself each day/week/month, whatever works for you. It may be taking a walk in nature, having a bubble bath or massage, enjoying a latte, spending time in stillness, going to personal development workshops or retreats, etc.

Relationships – Family is our support system, so make an effort to spend time with the family. Your children need you for their sense of belonging and feeling secure in their life. Try to mend any relationship issues you have with members of your family. Have healthy boundaries by being clear about your needs. Communicate your needs truly and honestly. Have no expectations and do not make assumptions.

Health – Choose some form of exercise or physical activity that you enjoy. It may be dancing, swimming, yoga etc. Eat fresh food as much as you can. Get enough rest and sleep.

Social – It is a well-known fact that having a social network helps to keep us happy. Do keep in touch with friends; go out doing things you enjoy. Maybe join a club with like-minded people or go out for dinner or theatre or dancing.

Work – Do the work you enjoy doing. Find work related to your passions. By following your purpose you make a difference to the lives of others. You may be a parent looking after your children; that is also a full-time job, so know that you still have worth. I know of some mothers who feel guilty if they are not working to earn money.

Contribution – Give in some way; it can be physically, of your time, by volunteering or giving of your knowledge to family, at school, a social club. It could be financial donations.

Spiritual – This can be taking a walk in nature, doing meditation, prayers, connecting with your higher self, the divine or God. Listen to your intuition.

Finances – If you are experiencing lack or hardship, then you may need expert advice. It may be that you have a perception of not having enough, when you actually do have your basic needs met. If you want more holidays or a better house you can practise gratitude for what you already have and create a vision board for what you would love to attract in your life, then let go of the outcome and let the Law of Attraction do its work.

'Never get so busy making a living that you forget to make a life.'

– Dolly Parton

Reflection

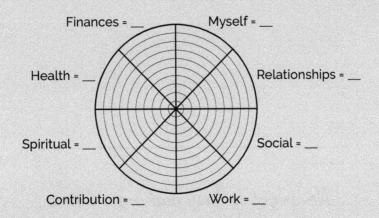

Finances = __   Myself = __

Health = __   Relationships = __

Spiritual = __   Social = __

Contribution = __   Work = __

Insert in the diagram the areas that feel relevant to your life at the moment.

In order to assess yourself, give yourself a grade for each area of your life, between 0 and 10, 0 being you do not spend any time doing this to 10 you spend a lot of time on it.

Which are the ones you are spending the least time on, and are areas of your life you would like to pay more attention to?

_____

_____

_____

Create an intention or a goal for one of the areas, for example 'I have decided to exercise 3 times a week'.

_____

_____

_____

Write the actions you need to take – e.g. Look for a swimming pool in my area.

_____

_____

_____

When will you take this action – e.g. Monday at 10 am.

_____

_____

_____

How will you take the action – e.g. Do swimming this Sat from 2 to 3 pm.

_____

_____

_____

What support will you need if any – e.g. Someone to look after the children?

_____

_____

Who will support you? Is there a family member to mind the children?

_____

_____

_____

What will be the benefits of doing this?

_____

_____

_____

CHAPTER TWELVE

Freedom to be still

'It is simply sitting silently, witnessing
the thoughts passing before you. Just
witnessing—, not interfering, not even
judging, because the moment you judge you
have lost the pure witness. The moment
you say "this is bad, this is good" you have
already jumped onto the thought process.'

– Osho

Stillness is a way to calm the mind. It is about awareness of the present moment of whatever you are doing. It is an activity where there are no other distractions to the mind. It simply means 'cessation of thought process'. It is a state of consciousness when the mind is free of thoughts. It is said that we have 65,000 thoughts a day, and if we create a gap between those thoughts, that moment of silence, that is stillness. It is the space between the notes that creates the music. Other words used for stillness are meditation, mindfulness, centring, grounding, prayers, and there are maybe more.

Studies have shown that mindfulness slows down the brain waves and this has been shown to increase the level of serotonin, a hormone which makes us feel peace and happiness. In an article on Harvard Medical School's blog, psychiatrist Dr Elizabeth Hoge[16] says that mindfulness can help people with anxiety by enabling them to recognize when they are having those negative, unproductive thoughts. They then know that it is simply a thought and nothing more.

We are living in a world of constant noise. Right now where I am sitting I can hear construction noise, sirens, cars driving past, television, and social media. This all keeps our minds busier than ever before. This constant doing does not give our mind any rest. Hence we find it hard to keep calm, to be focused, and we can even lose our creativity and productivity.

Why people don't meditate

The word meditation has often scared people because there is this idea that meditation is about sitting cross-legged for hours without any thoughts, so they feel they don't have time or that they can't do it. I am very pleased to hear that some schools are teaching mindfulness and yoga now. I do believe the earlier we start the better it is, as we all know childhood learning and habits stay with us in our adult life.

I have had so many people say to me 'I cannot meditate because I can't stop my thoughts'.

There is a misconception that we should be able to stop our thoughts completely for long periods of time in order to meditate. This cannot happen. To begin with the mind needs something to focus on so in meditation you choose what you want to focus on. You might focus on listening to your breath or your heartbeat or you may even listen to a guided meditation, all of which takes your focus from outside to you and your inner world.

Many people feel they do not have time to meditate, but meditation can be done anywhere and any time where you can become aware of your breath, or bring 100% focus on what you are doing. Meditation can even happen at night, as there is evidence that relaxation through meditation and a good night's sleep are the same thing. Some even suggest that the rest one gets from meditation is much deeper than sleep, as the brain waves during meditation are at the lowest level.

I had a client who had a very busy life. She was working full time and had two children, a husband and a home to look after. She felt she did not have time. Through the coaching she felt she really wanted to meditate, as she could see the value in it. As we started to explore where she could find the time, she found the time on the train whilst travelling to work. It took her 45 minutes to get to work so she said she would spend the first 10-15 minutes with her eyes closed and just focusing on her breathing. The rest of the time she wanted to read. When we spoke after two weeks, she reported back that she had managed to keep up the practice. At the beginning of the coaching she had said that she got very frustrated with the way her boss worked. Now since the meditation practice she felt that his behaviour just went over her head and did not bother her anymore.

I have been practising meditation for many years now. It was not easy at first, as I was so much in my head. I used to get frustrated and unhappy because I thought I did not do it properly and I was a failure. I had lots of thoughts, but with practice I seem to have longer periods of focus and there is sometimes a brief moment of complete focus where it feels very peaceful. Some days the focus is great and other days it is not. I have learnt not to judge myself. The fact that I sat and did the practice is good enough. Even when

I have the intention of doing the meditation and I don't do it, I have learnt to forgive myself.

I find the day very calm on the days when I do my meditation practice. I don't get so upset or frustrated. I have also noticed during my meditation that some of the thoughts I have are reflective thoughts from the previous day. I will notice my actions; a particular one I remember was that I may have come across as very rude to a friend of mine whom I had spoken to the day before. With this insight I was able to apologize to her the next time I saw her.

I often get ideas for my workshops during my meditation, so I believe that all thoughts are not to be ignored in meditation. It has allowed to me to listen to my intuition. Recently I have had many insights about what to say to my children about family issues that have upset me, and I know that these thoughts are from my soul and not my ego, so they come from a place of love and not fear or judgments.

Without the practice of meditation and stillness, you are lowering your chances of reflection, deep rest, better health and divine connection.

How to develop stillness

With any style of meditation or stillness you may find your mind has wandered. Without judgment you just come back to the thing you are focusing on. Whether it is mindfulness, meditation or stillness. The great thing is that you can practise stillness anywhere and for as little as a few seconds to several hours. Even at traffic lights, as I have often heard Dr Wayne Dyer say in the audios of his live lectures as a joke, but it is so true. He said, When you stop at the red lights, you can close your eyes and meditate, and when they turn green, the person behind you is bound to honk, to let you know that it is time to move on. Sometimes people say they cannot practise at all at work, as it would be against work culture.

I say to them, there are always the washrooms you can disappear to. As I said, you can practise anywhere.

Practise the ones that fit in with your life. It may be that you do short ones when feeling the need to quiet the mind and the longer ones when you have time. Do the ones you enjoy the most. The last thing you want is to get stressed over it.

Breathing

Focusing on your breathing can be done with closed or open eyes, and anywhere, whilst driving, walking, working etc. Listen to your breath, and notice where are you in your attention and be still with your breath for as little as a few seconds and notice the difference.

I often focus on breathing deep into my abdomen, imagining I am filling a balloon in my stomach and breathing out all of the stale air in my lungs. I do this for a few moments when I am feeling tired and it energizes me. I also practise this breathing when I feel my mind is too busy, especially if I have company and I have been talking a lot.

Chakras

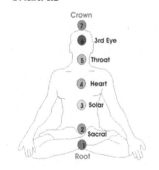

By LordtNis - Own work, CC BY-SA 4.0, https://commons.wikimedia.org/w/index.php?curid=47747148

There are seven major energy centres in the body as per the diagram shown. Focusing on each centre is not only a great meditation, but it is also a way of balancing the body, mind and soul as each chakra is related to our physiology and emotional state. You can start by focusing on each centre for a few minutes or so. You may start from the first one at the base and move up. I do this in the shower sometimes, and other times when I cannot get to sleep. I start from the top to the base in order to bring the energy down.

Mindfulness

Mindfulness means focusing and being 100% present and you can practise it with everyday tasks like washing up, walking, or listening to soothing, calming music. Using the five senses, which are touch, smell, hearing, sight, and taste, become conscious and be present to what you are doing. Again when you realize the mind has wandered, just come back to being present. Notice what you notice and be present to smells, texture and the stillness.

One I personally like is to feel the energy between my palms. About 10 years ago I was introduced to Dhan yoga, which was founded by Ilchi Lee, from Korea. At the end of the class we place both our palms facing each other in front of our chest. You can do it by focusing your attention between your palms with eyes closed and when you feel the energy, like warmth, or a magnetic sensation, then as you breathe in you can expand the energy by moving the palms apart and as you breathe out you bring your palms together.

At first I was finding it very difficult to feel anything as I was using my left brain to analyse the 'how' of it. After two months when I let go of my thinking and just focused on the energy I started to feel a magnetic field between my palms. Once I stopped wanting to know how to do this correctly and just accepted how it felt each time, I got deeper and deeper into it. Now I can almost instantly get into a quiet mind and feel the energy. After the class I feel really calm and also feel a lot of peace.

This is a great one for children to help them to feel calm, and helps with concentration as well.

Visualizing

Visualize your favourite holiday place where you can relax. It could be seaside and beach, or hiking, or whatever is fun and relaxing and rejuvenating for you. Just a few minutes of this when you are feeling stressed at work can work wonders. If you find it hard to visualize, create a vision board or look through holiday photos to bring back the emotions and feelings associated with those times in your life when you felt still and at peace.

Mantras

Silently repeat a mantra, which is a word which can be linked with one of the names of the divine like 'om' or even words like 'peace' or 'love'.

I started practising meditation with a mantra that I repeat silently in my mind. I try to do a daily practice of very early morning meditation, at between 4 and 5 in the morning. I understand for divine connection that is the best time as there is the least amount of negative energies around us. As I repeat my mantra I imagine myself as a white light, becoming one with the whole of the universe.

Guided meditations

Here is a link www.azminajiwa.com/resources to a guided meditation that you can listen to. Being guided in a meditation is very useful if you are a beginner or find it hard to focus on your own.

Benefits of meditation

> Meditation gives you better focus, as stillness is about focusing on one thing, so this practice helps us to focus better in other areas of our life. This in turn improves efficiency and creativity. A greater degree of focus improves the memory as well.

> You should have less anxiety because as you meditate regularly the neural pathways in the brain change; there is reduced activity in the amygdala, the part of the brain that processes emotional stimuli, and therefore you do not react as strongly to past fears.

> You are calmer and more at peace, so your response to irritations in life, which would normally create frustrations or anger, would instead be calmer and with compassion. You will be more in the flow of life and you will have more energy.

> You will be able to reflect on past actions and also get ideas for any future projects. We get an opportunity to listen to our intuition which is our inner guidance system.

> You will have better health, because meditation lowers the heart rate and blood pressure. The body heals quicker from the deep rest.

> You may feel a closer connection to God, the divine, a higher self, soul, or whatever you like to call that energy.

'Meditation can help us embrace our worries, our fear, our anger, and that is very healing. We let our natural capacity of healing do the work.'

– Thich Nhat Hanh

Reflection

Have you practised any meditation so far?

If yes –

Have you been able to sit still?

_____

How did it feel to be still?

_____

_____

_____

Where you able to just observe your thoughts?

_____

_____

_____

What benefits have you derived from your practice?

_____

_____

_____

If no –

Which method do you feel would suit you best?

_____

_____

_____

When would be the best time for you to practise?

_____

_____

_____

CHAPTER THIRTEEN

Freedom to tell your story

'Our greatest happiness does not depend
on the condition of life in which chance
has placed us, but is always the result of a
good conscience, good health, occupation,
and freedom in all just pursuits.'

- Thomas Jefferson

In order to truly hear yourself and capture your thoughts, you often need to be able to tell your story, the whole story, without censoring or editing your thoughts and feelings.

Sadly, very few people are able to listen to your whole story especially when you are stuck in the part of your story where you feel hopeless, worthless and like there is no hope.

When you apply the tools and processes I have shared in this book you will over time update your story. Where there was pain there will be learning and where there was despair there will be hope as you gain an understanding of what the tough times taught you, and then you can tell your story from a place of strength and confidence.

That is when it is easier for others to listen to the whole story.

Writing this book gave me the space and time to delve deeper into the stories I had told myself and it allowed me to update more of my thoughts and beliefs that were no longer serving me.

I found myself unsure how much of my personal story to tell you in this book and yet I know that I have read books where someone has taught me the process and I finished the book not feeling like I knew them at all.

Through the process of writing this book I have benefited from sharing my story with my book mentors, editor, peer review team, family and friends who read, gave feedback and listened to my story.

I was asked questions like, what kind of never? Or what kind of always? And with every discussion I became more and more aware of all the amazing things that I have achieved in my life that had been overlooked and not fully embraced because I was so busy suppressing those feelings that I didn't know how to express.

As I learned to tell my story I discovered that things were often not as bad as I thought and it reminded me of how much I had achieved despite how I felt at the time.

When we have the courage to share our story we usually discover that we are not alone in our thinking and that the journey we are all on is very similar and normal.

And depending on who you tell and who you listen to, you can often discover that when life isn't how you would like it to be then you can change it. It is your life and you are in control.

The problem with not telling your story is that it can become distorted and out of perspective when it is left inside, untold and therefore unchallenged by you or others. It can eat away at your soul, leaving you feeling unworthy. When you learn to look back on your journey so far and you look at how your life story has been unfolding there is often more wisdom than you can possibly imagine.

The key is stopping long enough to learn the lesson and then consciously deciding to write the next chapter of your life exactly how you would like it to be.

My journey started because I opened up to my brother who was a psychologist and he recommended a DVD, and that along with a book I had been reading inspired me to question myself and the thoughts I was having.

Perhaps you have a story, a feeling or even a book stuck inside you wanting to get out.

Throughout this book I have shared parts of my story, however if you would like to hear more about me and my story, I have shared it in the final chapter.

'To be yourself in a world
that is constantly trying to
make you something else is the
greatest accomplishment.'

— Ralph Waldo Emerson

Reflection

Take a moment now to write your life story.

_____

_____

_____

_____

_____

_____

_____

_____

_____

_____

_____

_____

_____

_____

_____

Think about 6 turning points in your life.

1. _____

2. _____

3. _____

4. _____

5. _____

6. _____

What did those turning points teach you?

_____

_____

_____

_____

When you do this activity again in 10 years' time, what will the story be then?

_____

_____

_____

_____

CHAPTER FOURTEEN

My story

'Today I choose life. Every morning when
I wake up I can choose joy, happiness,
negativity, pain... To feel the freedom
that comes from being able to continue
to make mistakes and choices – today
I choose to feel life, not to deny my
humanity but to embrace it.'

– Kevyn Aucoin

Childhood

I was born in Uganda, East Africa. My parents were Ugandan citizens. My grandfather came from Gujarat in India during the time when Uganda was a British colony. I was the eldest of seven children, all of whose names start with 'A'.

I don't remember a lot in the way of feelings and emotions from my childhood.

I have memories of there being a lot of emphasis on education. Asian and Indian families generally push their children to perform well academically and this can have a positive effect on some children and a negative effect on those that have different talents. I performed well academically whilst my sister was more talented with arts and drama; she was never encouraged and was often told off for following these interests.

I remember my father being very strict, and when he was angry with us he would lash out and hit us. I remember him hitting one of my sisters, as she was someone who would answer back, whereas I and another of my sisters would withdraw.

I remember my mum saying to us not to make a noise or bother Dad, as he would get angry.

Teens

As a teenager I was very shy. I was very self-conscious most of the time, feeling that everyone was watching me. I was very quiet at school. I hardly looked at boys and found it difficult to talk to them. I have met a few of my classmates in the last few years, and they cannot believe that I am the same person they knew at school. I have changed so much and have greater confidence now.

I did not want to go to birthday parties or school parties and yet my mum would make me. I would feel very awkward and embarrassed, to the extent that I did not even want to eat at the table if we had guests having dinner with us.

I was so afraid that I would do something wrong. What if I made a mistake? What if I appeared silly? What if I didn't know what to say?

What if? What if?

Of course, now I know there is no such thing as mistakes and failures. There are only outcomes, results or feedback. If we do and say something, which with hindsight was not acceptable, we can learn from it and behave differently next time.

At age of 16 I met Salim, who was 20 years old, and I guess we fell in love. I say guess, because I didn't really know what love was or know anything different, but we were definitely getting along.

We were not allowed to be with boys on our own in those days, as one's reputation would be tarnished, as you would be labelled as a loose girl. I must have had a daring side to me as I continued to meet him in secret, by telling my parents I was visiting my girlfriends. After a year he left to come to study in Scotland and we used to write to each other.

At the age of 17 I came to England, to get a better education myself; as I said earlier, education is very important to Indian families and there was only one university in Uganda.

Here I was in a completely new country, with no family, community or friends which I had been so used to. I felt very isolated and lonely. I was living with an English couple, Jack and Connie, in a town called Chatham in Kent.

I started to do 'A' levels at Medway Maidstone College. I was still very quiet and shy. I did not make friends easily. In the community I came from in Uganda, we all knew each other. So, for a shy person, you can imagine how out of my comfort zone I was. I only had one friend, and she was from Uganda as well. I remember once or twice a group of students, who I assume were ignorant about the history of Ugandan Asians, shouted out 'You Paki go home', which left me feeling like I didn't belong and inferior.

I was very conscious of this, and it made me feel very uncomfortable.

Though Connie and Jack were caring people, they were in their fifties and had no children of their own, so I felt that I had no one to share my story and feelings with.

I had just finished one year there when the 'Uganda Crisis' took place when all the Indian/Asian people had to leave Uganda. Everyone's bank accounts were frozen, so my parents could not send me my fees for college or my lodgings.

I was lucky that Jack and Connie were friends with one of my uncles, and they were kind enough to let me stay with them. Then my parents had to leave Uganda. They became refugees and were taken to camps in Italy.

For three months I did not hear from them. It was 1972. In those days it was not easy to use a phone, plus they did not have much money. Eventually when I heard from them, they were in the USA, where they were going to settle.

So now I did not have any money and neither did they, but as refugees the UK government and my faith community, known as Ismaili Muslims, were very helpful. My faith community was able to make arrangements with a bank to loan members of the community money for education.

Career

At this point I had to look for a profession I could enrol into with the science subjects I had from my GCSE. My choices were nurse, dental hygienist, physiotherapist and chiropodist. I went for chiropody, on the basis that I could be my own boss and I thought I would enjoy it, helping people to walk comfortably.

I went to the London Foot Hospital to study to be a chiropodist. I was living in a YWCA, sharing a dormitory with five other girls.

Luckily for me one of the girls, Carol, was also a new student at the Foot Hospital, so I felt a sense of comfort that I could walk into the school and would not be alone. I did make a couple of other friends in my year but not as many as I could have, as I was still very much lacking in confidence.

Over the holidays and evenings, I was mostly on my own, normally working, as I needed the money to feed myself and for other expenses. I was doing jobs like babysitting, working in the office in the evening, writing addresses on envelopes for a medical magazine company, cleaning and cooking breakfast in the hostel.

In the holidays I was the cleaner for the YWCA. Most people went home during the holidays, but I could not due to the fact my parents were not settled as yet and I did not have enough money to go to the States.

I remember feeling really proud when the matron of the hostel gave me a huge compliment: she said, 'You are little, but you have a lot of vitality'.

I am glad of all of these experiences although it was tough at times; sometimes I didn't even have enough money to buy a packet of chips which in those days were just five pence. Those experiences have made me very thrifty and this came in very useful later in life. When I got married, I was able to save and put up with not having furniture, a washing machine, and even a fridge for the first year. I guess that makes me patient and resilient as well.

As I write this part of my story I can now see that even then I had some great qualities in me, doing all kinds of jobs to make ends meet. Looking back, I describe myself as being resourceful, but I did not appreciate myself then as I do now. I am much happier now that I appreciate my good qualities. It is not selfish or boasting, as we are led to believe when we are little. I am also curious to notice how resourceful I am still today even though I don't have to do all those things. This is the power of telling your story. You get to check what you are saying and thinking and you just keep learning and growing.

In July 1975 I qualified as a chiropodist, which is now known as a podiatrist, and in September of the same year at the age of 22, I got married to Salim.

Marriage

I never dated anyone else apart from Salim. When I look back I would say it was because of low self-esteem and it was easier to stay in my comfort zone, and yet now I also know that fate was playing its part and we were meant to be.

As I mentioned earlier, phoning each other was not so easy. At the end of his holiday he decided to come and see me before going back to Scotland where he was studying to be a pharmacist. So he came to Chatham, thinking he would ask at the college for my address.

As he was walking up the hill, I was coming down the hill to go down to the town and we came face to face with each other, so I believe it was our destiny and a divine connection between us.

We had some mutual friends, mainly from my faith. I was still very conscious that I was not English and felt I did not belong.

In many ways I was still shy; for example I would not go across a pedestrian crossing unless someone else was crossing with me. I felt self-conscious and did not want to put anyone out just for me. I was not important and yet life was fun. Both of us worked, six days a week, and we shared the housework. We used to have three holidays a year. Generally we enjoyed the same activities, like swimming, walking and travelling.

My confidence level was a little better than before. I think that was because I felt I was somebody, now that I had a profession, and I could proudly tell people what work I was doing.

Children

After four years of marriage I had our two children. Of course, as soon as a child is born there is that moment of pure joy when you see and hold them. But like many parents I did my best even though I was still not emotionally connected and free to be me. I was drowning in fear and that, I believe, meant that I was not as able to connect to myself or my children as well as I can today. Now I see the gift my children have been and all they have taught me about myself and life.

Because of our children, I started to have a different life, in the sense that I would take the children out and meet up with other parents and their children. This is when my fear of rejection, and fear of getting things wrong, became more apparent.

In addition to this my husband would comment on the fact that I was not home when he returned for lunch, saying something like 'I don't like coming home to an empty house' or 'Where were you?' This resulted in me gearing all of my activities around being there to please him and less and less listening to my own needs and wants. I would find myself telling friends that I couldn't come because my husband wouldn't like it and sometimes I even said 'He won't allow me'.

Now that I know about how our childhood experiences influence us, it makes sense of why he would have felt alone and why I felt as though I had to change to please him.

My childhood and of course my natural way of being meant that I was shy, timid, and wanted to please people like my mum.

I suspect the fear came from the fact that my dad was quite a forceful personality. When he questioned me or commented, it felt like a command and my mum was fearful, so I suspect I learned that behaviour too.

With this in mind it showed up in my marriage as me believing that I had to be home otherwise I would be told off and he might reject me. If Salim left any tasks for me to do like posting letters, or some paperwork that he needed help with, instead of communicating with him assertively and positively, I just accepted and apologized, and also felt terrible about not having been more efficient.

On my journey I have learnt that people will treat you the way you allow them to.

Treadmill of life

Like a lot of people, I got in what I call the treadmill of life: I would get up, get the kids to school, do the housework, pick up the kids, cook etc.

In between all of the good stuff like going on holiday, being confident with close friends, there were still those moments of not feeling good enough. I would have to keep pushing down those thoughts and beliefs of self-doubt, worthlessness and fear so that I could get back on the treadmill, without really dealing with how I was feeling.

I was focusing on what was best for the children or my husband and when it came to me I was only really focusing on the essentials like getting my hair cut. I was still being critical of myself; doing what others wanted became a way of life and it also became my comfort zone. I was not happy, but I was comfortable. I realize now that I had lost the sense of who I was and when I was asked what

I liked, I really did not know. I was often just describing what my husband liked.

And there were some things I did in spite of the fear, like attending a weekend course to train as a teacher in our faith. I was inspired enough to get over the fear. I had a feeling inside that this role would give me a sense of purpose and fulfilment. I think even then I knew I was meant to teach.

Light bulb moment

When my children were five and six years old I started to notice that they were not very confident either. At least I had the wisdom to recognize at this stage that I was contributing to their low self-esteem and lack of security, so in 1985 I attended a brilliant course on parenting, and this was my first conscious experience of a transformation.

This 12-week course of two and a half hours per week helped me to deal with some of my own fears and taught me how to be with my own children.

I also stopped labelling them as bad or good, just commented on the behaviour. I allowed them to learn from their own mistakes and gave them praise more than criticism. My daughter even today can remember how differently she felt when I started to notice what they were doing well. My son says he has learnt to be positive in life and that is helping him to be successful.

The course also taught me a lot about communication, which really helped me to communicate differently with my husband.

Despite these massive improvements for my children and their confidence, some nine years later I was still struggling with my own confidence.

At the age of 41 I was appointed as a board member in a committee in my community. This was a voluntary commitment. It was considered to be a prestigious position, as not everyone gets that opportunity. Half way through my term of three years, I began to feel quite intimidated and under confident. I found myself putting other people on a pedestal. At the time I did not acknowledge that the portfolio I was given was because I was the best person for it, as I had the most experience in that particular area. In our board meetings I would back down too soon; I would not put my point across as I would have liked to.

Menopause

By now the hormonal changes were also destabilizing the 'norm' that I had created, which involved ignoring my own feelings and focusing on others as a priority. I wasn't able to talk to anyone because I knew from the outside I looked as though I should have nothing to complain about. Materially I had everything one could wish for. So the only way to change things was to go within.

First, I started by reading and listening to DVDs. I remember a couple of books early on that talked about the menopause being a time for women to find themselves, to go within, and time for our spirituality to emerge. As I reflect I can now see how that was the case. I had pushed down all those feelings of low self-esteem and fear of rejection, and just got busy with doing, rather than being.

I did not want to feel bad and dealing with the feelings was too painful. And yet those feelings were surfacing during this time of the menopause, until eventually it became too hard to push them down any longer. I guess life was calling for me to deal with those suppressed feelings.

Although I took some medication for the palpitations, all the reading I had done brought me to the conclusion that the answers had to come from within, that happiness is from within oneself.

This gave me hope and I started to read more and more books in search of the answer. I also started to attend events. I wanted to learn all there was to learn about how to explore my own thinking.

Trainer and speaker

Then a leaflet came through the door about becoming a performance coach. I became curious as to what this was about and on inquiring further I found that it was about improving employee performance at work by making them feel good about themselves.

This seemed like something I would like to do and whilst I started the home study course with the purpose and intention of helping others it helped me to work on myself too.

Around the same time, I also went to a three-day seminar with Anthony Robbins where he gets the participants to do a lot of physical energy work, which I found very helpful. When I was not able to do the mind work, I would jump about and throw my arms up in the air and shout YES many times. This had an impact on my emotions and I would feel a little positive.

As a trainer I now know that our mind and body have a connection. Before doing the fire walk he got us to jump about and shout 'Cool moss cool moss', and to look up, and the next thing I knew was that I had walked on hot coals.

Yes, I actually walked over hot coals which is a great process for overcoming fears limited by your mind. To actually experience that you can walk on hot coals and not get burned because you didn't allow your mind to think about it was a completely new experience for me.

I started to regularly practise exercise and meditation and found a really great centre where they do Dhan yoga, which is a combination of stretches, body tapping and meditation. I believe to get to know yourself you have to take a holistic approach and work on everything from your mind to your body and soul. As I did more and more of this practice, I found it really helpful to calm me down and get me to listen to my intuition.

In my search for happiness I came across a one-day workshop called 'Zest for Life' by Dawn Breslin.

The first half of the morning was yet another emotional roller coaster for me. I was gazing into the eyes of a photo of myself as a baby, and I realized how I had forgotten who I was, and I was lost to me.

I could not stop crying for that loss. This carried on into a lovely visualization where I connected with my inner child and a mentor, who further revealed my uniqueness, my desires and my dreams.

By the afternoon I had many tools to move me out of feeling stuck, unhappy and fearful into really having joy – feeling that I was important, and I could create my own happiness.

What I have come to realize is that during meditation time, when I allow time for myself, I get very emotional and now I know those are tears of joy and they indicate to me that I am now connected with my soul. Whereas before this training I was fearful and I would stop myself and just wouldn't go there.

When we came to the goal setting part of the workshop, I knew that I wanted to become a trainer, to share this new learning to help others to learn these simple skills to be HAPPY.

Although I knew at that point that I would love to become one of Dawn Breslin's trainers, when we were sharing our goals in threes the other participants noticed that I was saying 'I don't know if my husband would allow me'. This way of thinking and being had become such a habit that I did not even realize I was still saying this aloud.

I said to Dawn that I could not possibly do it that year, knowing very well that it was an excuse, so I didn't have to face my fear. I could actually feel my heart palpitations as I was thinking about wanting to do the workshop.

I must mention here that although in the earlier days my husband was not happy and he used to sulk and reject me for a while, if I did go away, I was lucky that his love for me was greater than his ego, or his insecurity, and of course he was also changing a little too.

As I used the tools I learnt in the workshop I became stronger, and more confident in myself, and nearer the time of the training I was able to say to my husband that I was going to go away for five days' training in Scotland, and to my surprise, he was fine about it.

The first day my heart was feeling so heavy because of the fear of what might happen when I went back home. I was worried about how Salim would react because I was away, and to my new behaviour and thoughts. Then I got excited that I was doing this for myself and that then turned into overwhelm as I realized just what was possible and how much could change.

Out of the five days I was very tearful for almost three days and many of those tears were of joy and a sense of connection that I had not had for so long.

At the end of the fifth day, I was on such a high that when I got back from Scotland on the train, my husband and children were there to pick me up, and they could see me really glowing, and so happy. My husband even said, 'You can go more often if it makes you this happy.'

After that I did a certificate and diploma in Life Coaching, then went on to became a neuro-linguistic programming practitioner (NLP). I started to run small group workshops on 'Zest for Life' as a Dawn Breslin trainer. The motivation and facing my fears came from the vision board we had created at the end of the workshop, with the time line of when I would hold my first trial workshop. It would have been very easy to give up as most of the people I was asking to attend were not interested, although it was a free workshop, and I was telling them how it would change their lives. I guess this scared them, as they may not have been ready for change or maybe did not need any personal development. I then changed my story, and told them that I would really value their feedback as this was my first workshop. I got twelve participants and I finished the workshop three hours before time. Of course it was far from perfect, but I carried on running about four workshops a year.

I was finding it hard to do the bouts of marketing I needed to keep holding these workshops, which I loved doing, so one day I just said to the universe, God, please give me a ready-made audience. I believe the Law of Attraction got working. I noticed some information about becoming a licensed trainer for Dr Susan Jeffers' bestselling book, *Feel the Fear and Do It Anyway*.

I had read her book and absolutely loved it, so I applied to become a trainer. In the past I would not have applied; my critic would have said 'Who are you to be a trainer of this famous book?' But by now I had learnt to use positive affirmations, so I felt the fear and did it anyway. As one of the trainers I started to get participants from Susan's website, so I did not have to do a lot of marketing myself.

I continued running both the workshops and as part of my request to have ready participants, I was getting invitations to speak, and was noticing where I could offer to speak, hence I became a speaker, not only in the UK but abroad as well.

One of the places I put myself forward to speak is at the Mind Body Soul Exhibitions where my husband and I have a stand. His hobby is palm reading, although he is a pharmacist by profession. I attended one of Doreen Virtue's certificated tarot reading courses so I combine card reading and life coaching at the shows. I am also a trainer of Forgiveness workshops by Azim Khamisa, who teaches a 4-step forgiveness process.

I have many books and a huge collection of personal development CDs that have built on the learning of these early day workshops and courses and I have shared them with you in this book.

I am a firm believer in a holistic approach and I am really pleased to say that, keeping up with all the practices I talk about in this book, I feel so much happier, calmer and more at peace.

Sometimes people believe that there will be an end to the practices and then they will live. I have learnt that growth is a journey all through life and it is to be enjoyed. I still have my ups and downs.

Joys of grandchildren

I am now a grandmother of two lovely kids – they are also my teachers. I have been able to use what I have learnt, with their growth. I still have to face new doubts that come up as to whether I am guiding them in the right way or not, and I am learning to enjoy them and not be so conscious of being perfect.

Watching them grow is reinforcing my beliefs in how we as adults influence young minds, and also that they do come with innate personalities that make them who they are as individuals. I have noticed that they can use their intuition if we allow them to. I normally ask them what they think is the answer when they ask me questions and it is amazing to hear their answers.

Author

Writing this book has been a very interesting journey. I started writing for the first time in 2013, with no planning. I reached four chapters and then got stuck. I simply did not know how to progress. After two years I met Karen Williams, the Book Mentor at Librotas. I had a VIP day with her to plan the book; this, I am told, makes or breaks the book. This set me up to start writing.

I came up against fears of not being as good at writing as others. I started to have self-doubt, asking myself questions like who would want to buy my book, who am I to teach others, when I am not perfect.

My writing was very slow, but Karen was very kind and allowed me to go at my own pace. I did want to finish my book, but was procrastinating. I decided to join Karen Williams and Sheryl Andrews (the Strength and Solutions Detective) at their writing retreat in Spain.

I did not get as much writing done as I thought I would, but Sheryl helped me to face my demons with a few sessions of coaching. With ongoing support from her I have been much more motivated and was finally able to finish writing this book.

It gives me great pleasure to make a difference to the lives of others and they often teach me as much if not more than I teach them. I love running workshops, and speaking at various events, and each time I have to prepare to teach of course I get to learn the lesson all over again.

Afterword

I am humbled, grateful and really pleased to have written this book. The tools in this book have helped me in my ups and downs of life. Without the downs there is no appreciation of the ups just as there would be no appreciation of light if there was no darkness.

The freedom to take the next steps

It is my humble hope that this book gives you the tools to explore and use so that ultimately you are able to have the freedom to love and nurture your self.

It is my hope and prayer that by the end of reading this book you will find your purpose, express your potential and serve humanity. After all, we are born be happy and to share our gifts with others.

Praise your self often – you are amazing so acknowledge your greatness.

Forgive yourself often. Be willing to learn from what did not go as well as expected. Be kind to yourself by saying 'It's okay (your name), it's the only way I knew how at that moment and time.'

These tools will, I hope, keep you in high energy and spirits. You will be happy – peaceful and fulfilled.

I would love to hear your story and how you get on with the book. You can email it to me at azmina@azminajiwa.com.

After reading the book, if you would like to delve deeper into the journey of freeing yourself from what's limiting you, then I would love to hear from you. Feedback I have had from participants who have attended my workshops on 'Feel the Fear and Do It Anyway'® is that just reading the book for them was not enough motivation to actually do the exercises, and therefore attending the workshop, where they had the opportunity to share experiences and challenges, and also have support from a trainer, made a big difference in their transformation.

I will be running one-day workshops and shorter sessions over several weeks, that will take you on a journey of Freedom to be YOU. I also help individuals who would prefer one-to-one sessions.

Get in touch with me to find out more on my website azminajiwa.com.

About the Author

*A*zmina Jiwa, a mum of two and grandmother to two, was born in Uganda, East Africa, in 1953. Her parents were Ugandan citizens; her grandfather came from Gujarat in India to Uganda during the time when it was a British colony. She was the oldest of seven children, all with names that start with 'A'. She recalls a lot of emphasis on education, which is typical within the culture of Asian and Indian families who push for their children to perform well academically.

Her memories of her childhood are limited but she does remember her dad having a temper and her mum encouraging them to keep quiet to keep the peace. Her sister, who was more outspoken, often got hit whereas she and her siblings would choose to withdraw.

At the tender age of seventeen Azmina moved to England to further her education as there was only one university in Uganda. Not long after this the Ugandan crisis happened and her parents found themselves refugees, with bank accounts frozen and being shipped to camps in Italy and finally settling in the USA. This left Azmina alone in England to fend for herself.

During this time Azmina, a shy and timid but resourceful girl, was left to face many differences and changes. There was so much about England that was different and she no longer had her family and local community to support her. For many years she felt that she didn't belong and that she was not good enough.

But she was not completely alone as her childhood sweetheart from Uganda had moved to Scotland for his education and they had stayed in touch. They have now been married since 1975.

Her confidence grew when she qualified as a chiropodist and felt she was now somebody as she had a profession and she was consciously aware of the difference she was making.

Then as Azmina hit the menopause it was as though the emotions that had been suppressed and unprocessed through the many changes in her life were crying out to be released. That is when her journey to discover her true self began and she started to learn how to have the freedom to be her. This book is her record of events, books, tools, seminars and workshops that inspired her to transform her thoughts, which in turn transformed the way she felt about herself and her life. She went from feeling that she was just existing on the treadmill of life to feeling inspired and living a life with purpose on purpose.

Today Azmina is a qualified coach, Feel the Fear and Do It Anyway and Zest for Life trainer and Neuro-Linguistic Programming Practitioner. She also has a certificate in tarot card reading by Doreen Virtue and is a trainer of Forgiveness workshops taught by Azim Khamisa.

She spends her time speaking, running workshops and writing to inspire and empower others who are experiencing change to go within and change the way they are thinking to change their lives.

References

1. David R. Hawkins, M.D., Ph.D. (2002), *Power vs Force – The Hidden Determinants of Human Behavior*, Hay House, Chapter Three, p. 70.

2. David R. Hawkins, M.D., Ph.D. (2002), *Power vs Force – The Hidden Determinants of Human Behavior*, Hay House, Chapter Three, pp. 68-69.

3. Susan Jeffers, Ph.D. (2012, revised edition), *Feel the Fear & Do It Anyway*, Penguin Random House UK, pp. 169–170.

4. Dawn Breslin is the founder of Harmonizing and author of *Guide to Super Confidence*.

5. 'A Theory of Human Motivation' in *Psychological Review*, 50, 370–396, accessible at: http://psychclassics.yorku.ca/Maslow/motivation.htm

6. Anthony Robbins' six core needs, https://www.habitsforwellbeing.com/6-core-human-needs-by-anthony-robbins/

7. Susan Jeffers, Ph.D. (2012, revised edition), *Feel the Fear and Do It Anyway*, Penguin Random House, p. 30.

8. Susan Jeffers, Ph.D. (2012, revised edition), *Feel the Fear and Do It Anyway*, Penguin Random House, p. 124 ('No Loss Model').

9. Dr Brené Brown (2012), *The Power of Vulnerability*, Sounds True.

10. Dr Brené Brown (undated), as quoted on the Taking Charge website of University of Minnesota, https://www.takingcharge. csh.umn.edu/daring-be-vulnerable-brene-brown

11. Sheryl Andrews (2017), *Manage Your Critic – From Overwhelm to Clarity in 7 Steps*, Step by Step Listening, p. 167.

12. Dr Gerard Hodgkinson, quoted on Nature & Health website, http://www.natureandhealth.com.au/news/cultivate-your-spidey-sense#5voxiQdjJ4RveY1S.99

13. London School of Business and Finance research, available at https://www.lsbf.org.uk/press-and-media/news-about-lsbf/2015/september/lsbf-careers-report-finds-that-47-of-uk-workforce-want-a-career-change

14. Wayne Dyer (2001), *10 Secrets to Success and Inner Peace*, Hay House, pp. 21 & 22.

15. Susan Jeffers, Ph.D. (2012, revised edition), *Feel the Fear and Do It Anyway*, Penguin Random House, pp. 154–155.

16. Dr Elizabeth Hoge (2014) quoted in Julie Corliss, 'Mindfulness meditation may ease anxiety, mental stress', Harvard Health Blog, Harvard Health Publishing, available at https://www.health.harvard.edu/blog/mindfulness-meditation-may-ease-anxiety-mental-stress-201401086967